The mystery of the Ottoman

Harem

The mystery of the Ottoman Harem

İlhan AKŞİT
The Former Manager of the Palaces

AKŞİT KÜLTÜR VE TURİZM YAYINCILIK

Text : İlhan AKŞİT

Translated by : Reşat Dengiç

Graphics Design : Özer Kocatepe

Color Separation : Figür Grafik

Printed by : Seçil Ofset Ltd. Şti.
100 yıl Mahallesi Mas-sit Matbaacılar Sitesi
4. Cadde No:77 Bağcılar-İSTANBUL

Cağaloğlu Yokuşu Cemal Nadir Sokak Nur İş Hanı 2/4 34440 Cağaloğlu-İSTANBUL Tel: (0212) 511 53 85 - 511 67 82 Fax: (0212) 527 68 13

Contents

Preface

The State Osman Bey founded in 1299 became a world Empire and performed 624 years on the stage of the history. During its long life, 36 Sultans took stage; Some were very capable and brave and some others were proven insufficient within history.

As in the histories of other countries, the Ottoman history has got to be evaluated in itself according to the terms and conditions of its eras.

In the Ottoman Empire, where a men's dominance was inevitable, we face with some incredibly effective Harem women by all means. Those women when the Sultans failed to rule their country, took stage and became dominant in all government issues. The Harem where the Imperial women used to live in with a limited freedom was always misunderstood by those taking a look at it from outside as it kept its mystery for centuries.

To be able to illuminate the secret and the mystic part of the Harem, we have decided to print this book presenting various parts of it. To make it easier for the foreigners to undertand its essence, the Ottoman history is also presented along with the life in the Harem, too. Concubines (The Women Slaves), İkbals(Felicities), Kadınefendis (The wives of the Sultans), Valide Sultans(The Sultana Mothers) and Haremağaları (Eunuchs) are also presented under separate headings.

Aş the last settlers of the Palace revealed many things regarding the life in the Ottoman Palace in their books, we have mostly covered the Harem in the Topkapı Palace. We have also tried to make it easier for a foreigner by touring about the Harem at the end of this book.

İlhan Akşit
April 15ʰ 2000

The Ottomans

There passed only one thousand years A.C Selçuk Bey from the Kınık Tribe of the Oğuz Turks who had converted to Islam founded The Great Seljuk Empire and started to be the defender of the Islamic Caliphs. To achieve their goal they needed the Persian and the Anatolian lands and it wasn't long after had they invaded Persia. The Byzantine palace started to hear the sound of the horseshoes of the Turkish horsemen nearby. To defend themselves they sent out a big army to their eastern border. It was 26 August 1071 when the Byzantine emperor Romen Diogenes fought Alparslan, the sultan of the Seljuks in the Manzikert (Malazgirt) Plain. At dusk, the very same day the result of the war seemed to be clear. Seljuk armies decisively defeated the Byzantines. With this victory, Turks wide opened the gates to Anatolia. Turkish horsemen riding through this gate took over most of Anatolia and captured Nicaea, a town that had a political and religious importance for The Byzantines. The Sultan of The Seljuks appointed Süleyman, the son of Kutalmış as the Sultan of Anatolia due to his success in leading the Turkish army. So, Anatolian Seljuk State was founded the capital of which was chosen to be Konya. They brought in Anatolia a new atmosphere with their distinctive culture. By producing great art, they started an immense construction campaign taking the Pre-Anatolian cultures into consideration. They built schools, mosques, hospitals in cities like Sivas, Erzurum, Konya and ornamented those buildings with splendid crown gates. Besides, they connected their capital Konya to neighbouring towns by well-arranged, secure roads and they built

Two different paintings of Osman Bey, the founder of the Ottoman Dynasty.

caravansaries to set the security along those roads.

Because of the Mongol threat in Central Asia, Kayı tribe of The Oğuz Turks had to leave their homeland for good. Their caravan first arrived in Eastern Anatolia and stayed in Ahlat for some time. Some of them decided to go back while the rest in about 400 tents moved on towards West and arrived in Ankara dwelling in Karacadağ. At the time, the Anatolian Seljuk Empire was being ruled by Alaeddin Keykubat. When the Sultan was to set off for a war in Western Anatolia he called in the new comers to join in the army as raiders. So, the warriors of the Kayı tribe led by Ertuğrul Bey became a part of the Great Seljuk army. While Alaeddin Keykubat had to ride back because of the Mongol threat raising in the East, Ertuğrul Bey fought on and captured Söğüt and the vicinity. So, the Sultan of the Seljuks gave Ertuğrul Bey Söğüt to stay in the wintertime and Domaniç plateau to spend their summers. Kayı tribe finally had their own homeland in Anatolia. While they were settling in Söğüt, Alaeddin Keykubat, the Sultan of the Seljuks died and the Mongol threat in the East started to grow considerably. Finally, the Mongol hordes overran the Seljuks in Kösedağ in the year 1243 and captured Anatolia. While Anatolia was under the Mongol reign Ertuğrul Bey died in Söğüt in 1281 in his 90s.

His youngest son Osman, at the age of 23, was appointed as the Bey. Osman Bey who was honoured by being promoted from a subdivision Principality to the highest office continued the raids for the expansion of their lands. He married Mal Hatun the daughter of the Vizier of the Seljuks and increased his political power. After that, he married Bala Hatun, the daughter of Sheikh Edebali, the ritual leader of the area so, he was able to empower himself virtually too. While strengthening himself with those marriages he was expanding his borders by conquering castles

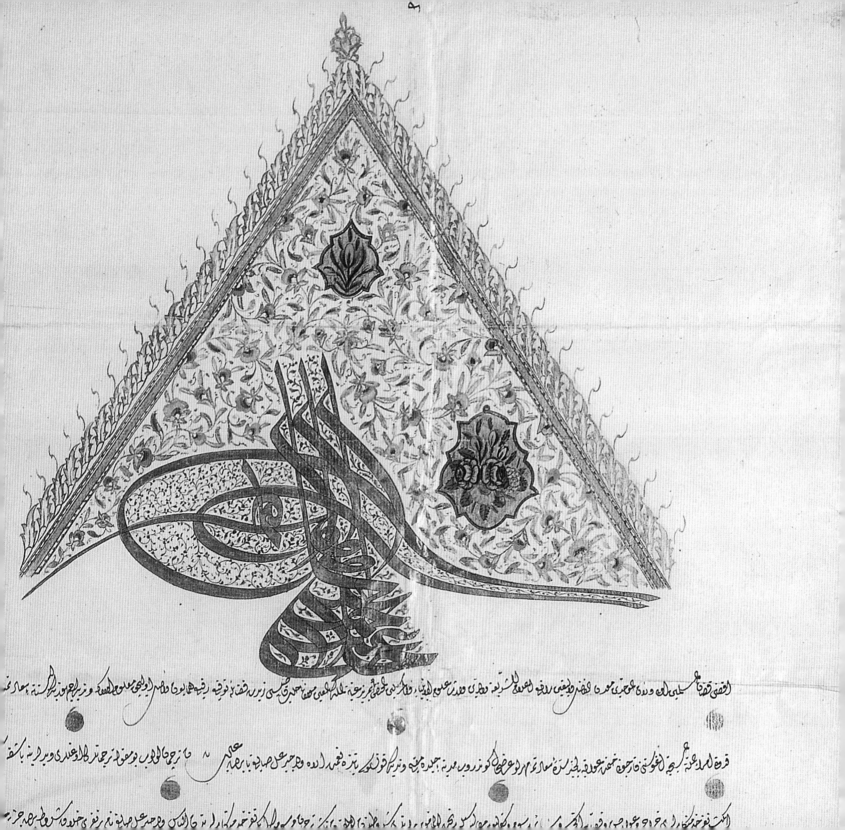

one after another. The neighbouring Byzantine princes were scared of his strength and considered him a potential danger. They were looking to find a way to kill him somehow. They planned to invite Osman Bey for a wedding ceremony and kill him there. Osman Bey soon found out what they had planned and he decided to retaliate their ambuscade attempt by falling them into ambush he was going to lay. He made his soldiers dress up in women's clothing and went for the wedding. When the Byzantines attempted to kill him his soldiers, taking off their fake clothing , put all the Byzantine soldiers and the princes to the sword. The bride Holifera , the daughter of Yerhisar prince left behind. Osman Bey married her to his son Orhan Bey and she converted to Islam later taking up a Turkish name; Nilüfer. During that time the Seljuk Sultans had no importance under the reign of The Mongols. Osman Bey, realising this fact, declared their independence. From then on, the dynasty was to be named by his name and called 'The Ottomans'. The Seljuk Empire already declined in 1308 not so long after his declaration of independence. So, many Principalities established in Anatolia gained their independence too. Osman Bey had the gout. Because of that everlasting illness he left his son Orhan Bey the reign of the Ottomans in 1324. He made a will and wanted his son Orhan Bey to capture Brusa (Bursa) at any cost and bury himself there. By his will, Orhan Bey reigning the Ottomans, took Brusa in 1326 and buried his father there who died at the age of 67.

That Ottoman Principality was to grow into the Ottoman Empire. The new ventures started taking place. Important steps were being taken to establish the departments of the state. From 400 tents there grew an army of 20.000 soldiers. While the Ottomans gaining power, their neighbours, the Byzantines were getting

A portrait of Sultan Mehmed the Conqueror painted by Sinan Bey.

The painting illustrating the conquest of Istanbul. Zonara, Dolmabahçe Palace.

P. Zonaro

weakened day by day by the fierce struggle over the throne. Princes trying to keep their thrones and avoid their enemies were begging Orhan Bey for his help. In such a case, The Byzantine emperor Andronikos III. asked for Orhan Bey's help and married his daughter Asporça to Orhan Bey in return. After that, John Kantakuzen VI who wanted Orhan Bey to be one of his relatives gave his daughter to him for a marriage. Orhan Bey after reigning for 36 years died in 1362 at the age of 80. His son Prince (Şehzade) Murad born from Nilüfer Hatun sat on the throne by the name Murad I.

Sultan Murad institutionalised the identification of becoming a state which Orhan Bey had earlier started. He secured the regulation in Anatolia and in 1362 by taking over Adrianople (Edirne) moved the capital there since it would be easier to rule his European conquests from there. Sırpsındığı and Çirmen victories made it easy for the Turks to move towards the heart of Europe. Thereupon, the Croats, the Hungarians, the Romanians, the Poles, and the Bulgarians gathered a crusades army of 100.000 soldiers and fought Ottomans in Kosova. Ottomans won a great victory against the crusaders. Unfortunately, Sultan Murad while walking about the battlefield got stabbed by a wounded Serb and so, the Turks lost a great ruler. Yıldırım Beyazıd, aged 29 ,born from Gülçiçek Hatun succeeded to the Ottoman throne in the battlefield. Yıldırım Beyazıd dominated Wallachia (Eflak) and defeated a huge crusaders army in Niğbolu. At that time he got married Devlet Şah Hatun, the daughter of Germiyanoğlu Süleyman Shah. For this political marriage, he was given Kütahya and the vicinity as a trousseau. The Serbian King Lazar I gave his daughter, Maria Olivera Despina to him to secure himself. Aydınoğlu İsa Bey was able to continue his Principality by giving his daughter, Hafsa

The armour ornamented with diamonds representing the glory of the Ottoman Empire grew from a small Principality.

Sultana to him.

After his victories in Europe, Yıldırım Bayezıd returned back to Anatolia and attacked the Turkish Principalities there. The rulers of the Principalities losing their lands fled to the Mongol Emperor Tamerlane's land for a protection, and the sultans of the countries invaded by Tamerlane came to Yıldırım Bayezıd to get sheltered. By their provocation, the two Turkish emperors fought. In the battle took place around Ankara in 1402, Yıldırım Bayezıd was defeated since the Principalities' soldiers who had been with him formerly decided to fight in favour of Tamerlane in the battlefield. Yıldırım Bayezıd became a prisoner of Tamerlane and died of his sorrow on 9 March 1403. Tamerlane remaining in Anatolia for 8 years went back to his homeland leaving a divided Anatolia in many pieces behind. Right after his departure from Anatolia a struggle over the throne started among the sons of Yıldırım. Mehmet Çelebi after a long struggle, re-founded the Ottoman Empire by defeating his brothers. His son, Murad II sat on the throne after his death in 1421.

Many problems were waiting for this young Emperor succeeded to the throne at the age of 18. Anatolian Principalities wanted to go back to their independent status before the Ankara Battle. That's why, Menteşoğulları, Germiyanoğulları, Aydınoğulları and Candaroğulları did not recognise Murad II and rebelled. At the same time, Murad II had to fight his uncle Mustafa and the brother Mustafa since they had rebelled together with the above mentioned Principalities too. Finally, he was able to reunion Anatolia in 1431. He had been reigning his country for 23 years. Although he was only 40 , the problems he had faced both in Anatolia and in Europe made him exhausted. That's why he left his throne to his son Mehmed II aged 12. But

The helmet ornamented with precious stones worn by the Ottoman Sultans belongs to the 16th. Century, Topkapı Palace.

since the Ottoman throne was left to a child, some movements started both in Europe and Byzantine and another Crusades army was prepared. Against that prominent danger Murad II took the Ottoman throne back again and left it to the son after defeating the Crusaders. And Murad II had to take the throne back once again when the janissaries (Yeniçeri) rebelled.

When the Sultan died on a winter day of 1451 in Adrianople (Edirne) Mehmed II who was going to be named The Conqueror (Fatih) later, succeeded to the throne. Sultan Mehmed the Conqueror (Fatih Sultan Mehmed) who sat on the throne at the age of 19, wanted Byzantine which was standing like an apex of a boil in the Empire, to be taken. He made his wishes come true by conquering Istanbul in 1453. Having conquered Istanbul, he moved the Capital to this city after Bursa and Edirne. He started to produce great art with a big construction

At the time of the Ottomans, sea transport was as important as that of the road. Public would take small boat trips and the sultans used the Sultanate boats.

16

campaign and beautified Istanbul.

Fatih returned back to Anatolia and captured Trebizond (Trabzon)Greek Empire , defeated Akkoyunlu State and expanded his lands as far as Crimea.

He died at the age of 49 as he set off for another war. His son Bayezıd II, a composer, a poet and a scientist sat on the throne. During his 31 year long sultanate, he took all precautions he found necessary to set the regulations and firmly establish the foundations of the Empire. Yavuz Sultan Selim who was quite enthusiastic found his father rather recessive and by dethroning him became the Sultan in 1512. He stopped the Shah Ismail rebellion his father always ignored before it created a big danger.

Yavuz Sultan Selim succeeded to the throne at the age of 42, which was quite an old age at the time to become a Sultan, attacked Egypt gaining the Islamic Caliphate to the Ottomans. After his

A painting by J. Brendesi illustrating the daily life in front of the Tophane fountain.

short but very successful sultanate of 8 years Yavuz Sultan Selim who was quite a sentimental poet at the same time, died in 1520 leaving his throne to his son Süleyman the Magnificient (Kanuni Sultan Süleyman) born of Hafsa Sultan.

The advancement era of the Ottomans reached its peak during his 46-year-long sultanate. After his long-lasting sultanate his son Selim II sat on the throne upon his death in 1566. Sultan Selim II who was in favour of peace never fought during his reign lasted for 8 years. He let Sokollu Mehmet Paşa deal with all the governmental affairs of the state while he devoted himself to religion and poetry. In the mean time, he ordered Architect Sinan (Mimar Sinan) to build the famous Selimiye Mosque in Adrianople (Edirne).

Selim II, who used to write poems using the name 'Selimi' left his throne to his son Murad III in 1574. We notice that Mehmed III replaced Murad III upon his death and Ahmed I succeeded to the throne after Mehmed III in 1603. That Sultan had the Ahmed I Has room constructed in the Harem.

Ottoman Empire had its most powerful era around the end of the 16th. century which would be followed by an arrested development era lasting until the end of the 17th. century. During that period, since The Empire was ruled by politically weak Sultans, and the women of the palace intervened in the government affairs and on top of everything the corruption of the army ended the glorious victories leading them to a decline in the 17th. century. The Sultans of the period respectively; Ahmed I, Mustafa I, Osman II, Murad IV, Ibrahim, Mehmed IV, Süleyman II, Ahmed II, Mustafa II, ruled the Empire. By the end of the 17th. century, although they had experienced a long troublesome era they were still one of the strongest countries of the world. The Ottoman Empire had to lose some of its lands after unsuccessful wars ended up with the signing of The Karlofça Treaty in 1699. The following 150 years became their retardation era. In that era, the Sultans ruled the Empire, respectively; Ahmed III, Mahmud I, Osman III, Mustafa III, Abdülhamid I, Selim III, Mustafa IV, continued to undertake the additional constructions in the Harem despite their huge land losses. Ahmed III's feast room, Osman III's mansion to be called by his name, Abdülhamid I.'s room for the favourite women, Selim III's two separate rooms one for himself and the other for his mother are reckoned as the additional buildings in the Harem. When Mahmud II born of Nakşidil Sultan started to spend his nights in palaces by the water, so, the Harem in the Topkapı Palace lost its previous glory. Abdülmecid, succeeded to the throne after him had the Dolmabahçe Palace built and moved there and of course, the Harem entirely lost its importance. After Abdülmecid, Abdülaziz sat on the throne being followed by Murad V's short reign. Abdülhamid II's sultanate which would last for a long period started afterwards. That Sultan did not prefer Dolmabahçe Palace and chose Yıldız Palace as his accommodation and lived there until he was dethroned in 1909. After him, Mehmed Reşat and Mehmet Vahidettin continued their sultanate in Dolmabahçe Palace. After taking a stage in history for 624 years with its 8 million square km. lands, 120 million inhabitants, dominating 38 countries in total, The Ottoman Empire completed its historical mission, and with the removal of Caliphate it collapsed on 3 March 1924 and was replaced by the young Republic of Turkey.

The portrait of Sultan Osman III, Topkapı Palace.

THE GENEAOLOGICAL TREE OF THE OTTOMAN DYNASTY

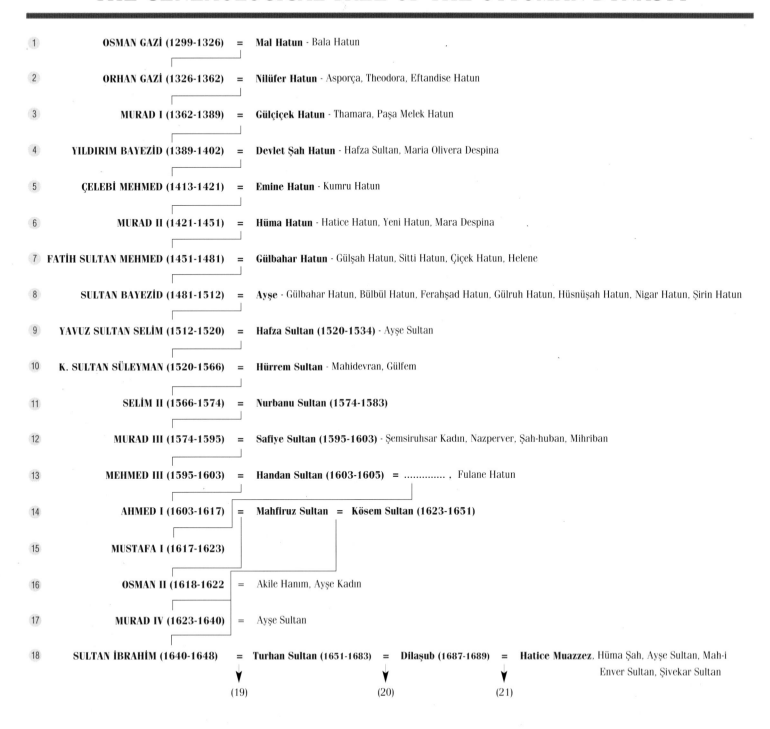

1. **OSMAN GAZİ (1299-1326)** = **Mal Hatun** - Bala Hatun

2. **ORHAN GAZİ (1326-1362)** = **Nilüfer Hatun** - Asporça, Theodora, Eftandise Hatun

3. **MURAD I (1362-1389)** = **Gülçiçek Hatun** - Thamara, Paşa Melek Hatun

4. **YILDIRIM BAYEZİD (1389-1402)** = **Devlet Şah Hatun** - Hafza Sultan, Maria Olivera Despina

5. **ÇELEBİ MEHMED (1413-1421)** = **Emine Hatun** - Kumru Hatun

6. **MURAD II (1421-1451)** = **Hüma Hatun** - Hatice Hatun, Yeni Hatun, Mara Despina

7. **FATİH SULTAN MEHMED (1451-1481)** = **Gülbahar Hatun** - Gülşah Hatun, Sitti Hatun, Çiçek Hatun, Helene

8. **SULTAN BAYEZİD (1481-1512)** = **Ayşe** - Gülbahar Hatun, Bülbül Hatun, Ferahşad Hatun, Gülruh Hatun, Hüsnüşah Hatun, Nigar Hatun, Şirin Hatun

9. **YAVUZ SULTAN SELİM (1512-1520)** = **Hafza Sultan (1520-1534)** - Ayşe Sultan

10. **K. SULTAN SÜLEYMAN (1520-1566)** = **Hürrem Sultan** - Mahidevran, Gülfem

11. **SELİM II (1566-1574)** = **Nurbanu Sultan (1574-1583)**

12. **MURAD III (1574-1595)** = **Safiye Sultan (1595-1603)** - Şemsiruhsar Kadın, Nazperver, Şah-huban, Mihriban

13. **MEHMED III (1595-1603)** = **Handan Sultan (1603-1605)** = ... , Fulane Hatun

14. **AHMED I (1603-1617)** = **Mahfiruz Sultan** = **Kösem Sultan (1623-1651)**

15. **MUSTAFA I (1617-1623)**

16. **OSMAN II (1618-1622** = Akile Hanım, Ayşe Kadın

17. **MURAD IV (1623-1640)** = Ayşe Sultan

18. **SULTAN İBRAHİM (1640-1648)** = **Turhan Sultan (1651-1683)** = **Dilaşub (1687-1689)** = **Hatice Muazzez**, Hüma Şah, Ayşe Sultan, Mah-i Enver Sultan, Şivekar Sultan

(19)   (20)   (21)

THE GENEAOLOGICAL TREE OF THE OTTOMAN DYNASTY

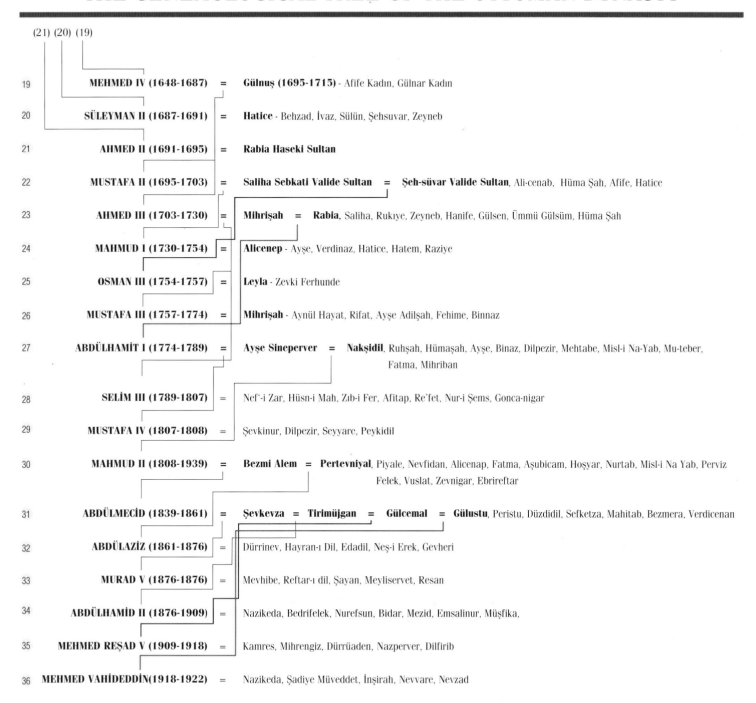

(21) (20) (19)

19   **MEHMED IV (1648-1687)** = **Gülnuş (1695-1715)** - Afife Kadın, Gülnar Kadın

20   **SÜLEYMAN II (1687-1691)** = **Hatice** - Behzad, İvaz, Sülün, Şehsuvar, Zeyneb

21   **AHMED II (1691-1695)** = **Rabia Haseki Sultan**

22   **MUSTAFA II (1695-1703)** = **Saliha Sebkati Valide Sultan** = **Şeh-süvar Valide Sultan**, Ali-cenab, Hüma Şah, Afife, Hatice

23   **AHMED III (1703-1730)** = **Mihrişah** = **Rabia**, Saliha, Rukıye, Zeyneb, Hanife, Gülsen, Ümmü Gülsüm, Hüma Şah

24   **MAHMUD I (1730-1754)** = **Alicenep** - Ayşe, Verdinaz, Hatice, Hatem, Raziye

25   **OSMAN III (1754-1757)** = **Leyla** - Zevki Ferhunde

26   **MUSTAFA III (1757-1774)** = **Mihrişah** - Aynül Hayat, Rifat, Ayşe Adilşah, Fehime, Binnaz

27   **ABDÜLHAMİT I (1774-1789)** = **Ayşe Sineperver** = **Nakşidil**, Ruhşah, Hümaşah, Ayşe, Binaz, Dilpezir, Mehtabe, Misl-i Na-Yab, Mu-teber, Fatma, Mihriban

28   **SELİM III (1789-1807)** = Nef'-i Zar, Hüsn-i Mah, Zıb-i Fer, Afitap, Re'fet, Nur-i Şems, Gonca-nigar

29   **MUSTAFA IV (1807-1808)** = Şevkinur, Dilpezir, Seyyare, Peykidil

30   **MAHMUD II (1808-1939)** = **Bezmi Alem** = **Pertevniyal**, Piyale, Nevfidan, Alicenap, Fatma, Aşubicam, Hoşyar, Nurtab, Misl-i Na Yab, Perviz Felek, Vuslat, Zevnigar, Ebrireftar

31   **ABDÜLMECİD (1839-1861)** = **Şevkevza** = **Tirimüjgan** = **Gülcemal** = **Gülustu**, Peristu, Düzdidil, Sefketza, Mahitab, Bezmera, Verdicenan

32   **ABDÜLAZİZ (1861-1876)** = Dürrinev, Hayran-ı Dil, Edadil, Neş-i Erek, Gevheri

33   **MURAD V (1876-1876)** = Mevhibe, Reftar-ı dil, Şayan, Meyliservet, Resan

34   **ABDÜLHAMİD II (1876-1909)** = Nazikeda, Bedrifelek, Nurefsun, Bidar, Mezid, Emsalinur, Müşfika,

35   **MEHMED REŞAD V (1909-1918)** = Kamres, Mihrengiz, Dürrüaden, Nazperver, Dilfirib

36   **MEHMED VAHİDEDDİN(1918-1922)** = Nazikeda, Şadiye Müveddet, İnşirah, Nevvare, Nevzad

The Harem

Meaning 'the home of happiness', Harem was the place where the guardian of the family lived in with his women, female slaves and the children. This place formed with the same structure in the palace used to be called Darüssaade (The home of happiness) earlier and named as the Harem in later years where the guardian was of course the Sultan himself.

Although the Ottoman Harem is famous, the Abbasides and the Seljuks used to have Harems too. The Sultans kept female slaves in their harem but they only married the daughters of the Christian princes in neighbouring countries and of the Principalities. But, that tradition changed after Bayezid II and the harem became a place where candidates could become the Sultan's wives were kept and selected afterwards. Except for a few, almost all the Sultans followed that tradition and married female slaves selected amongst the candidates in the Harem. When Sultan Mehmed the Conqueror took Istanbul in 1453, he beautified the city by having many works of art constructed. He had a palace built in Beyazid square after the palaces built in previous capitals, Brusa (Bursa) and Adrianople (Edirne). That palace was used for some time but a little later since they were in need of much room Topkapı Palace had to be built between 1472-1478 by Sultan Mehmed the Conqueror in order

to move the Sultanate to a much bigger location. The foundation of the Harem started with a few buildings by the golden road first. During the

The famous painting of jean-Léon Gérome, "Turkish Bath".

A concubine is putting on her clothes in the Harem, Théodere Chassériov.

construction work of the new Palace it turned to be a giant compound with the additional buildings within years. That new palace became a location where the governmental affairs were undertaken and a place for the Sultan's public procession greeting his public while going to mosque on Fridays. In the meantime, the old palace was used as the Harem. Although the Harem remained in the former palace Sultan Süleyman the Magnificent made use of Saray-ı Duhteran (The palace of the women) in the newly built Palace from time to time. It is often said that Hürrem Sultana moved to the Sultan's most favourite chamber and had a long lasting love affair with Süleyman the Magnificent. Structuring work continued in the Topkapı Harem until the period of Murad III. Murad III relocated the former Harem totally to the recently built Topkapı Palace in the year 1587 and so, it gained its importance once again. He also started to stay at the Murad III mansion Mimar Sinan had built. The Harem which was quite small at the time of Fatih Sultan Mehmed (Sultan Mehmed the Conqueror) advanced with the new additional compounds the following Sultans' ordered to be added. Unfortunately , this very well-developed Harem ruined by a big fire in 1665. After it was restored, The Istanbul earthquake hit that unique architecture and knocked it down in the year 1776. Having been restored once again, it was re-opened and continued its advancement with the additional compounds until the period of Mahmud II. In later years, Harem lost its previous magnificence as the palaces (so called the splendid villas) by the Bosphorus became much more popular. Of course the top stars of the Harem were the Sultans themselves. After the Sultan, came Valide Sultan (the Mother Queen-the mother of the Sultan). After his son sat on the throne, the Mother Queen would ride to the new Palace from the old one in a glorious parade accompanied by The Mother Guards and settle in the Mother's chamber. After Valide Sultans there came Kadınefendis, the wives of the Sultan having different titles like 1st., 2nd., 3rd. Kadınefendis and would live in separate chambers with their children. No doubt that the most colourful people of the Harem were the Cariyes(female slaves). Having been selected by the Sultan they would be able to obtain one of those titles. The unselected female slaves would remain in the Harem and undertake various duties.

There was another class formed in the Harem called Haremağaları who were in charge of the security affairs of the Harem. We understand how important their title was by checking the protocol queue; Darüssaade Ağası (The head of the Harem security) would take the third row in the queue coming after Sadrazam (The Grand Vizier) and Şeyh-ül-Islam (The head of the Islamic hierarchy).

Now, let us start to get to know the life in the Harem along with its people in details by revealing the secrets as much as possible.

The women Slaves

Cariyelik (Women slavery) goes back to the era before Islam. Baghdad used to be the most important slave market at the time of the Abbasides. After Islam this business had to continue due to social and economic factors.

We notice that women slavery in the Ottoman Harem started with Orhan Bey, but from the period of Sultan Mehmed the Conqueror the number of women slaves in the Harem increased rapidly. Starting from the middle of the Bayezid II's period, the tradition of the Sultans' marrying the neighbouring princelets' and Principalities' daughters ended . After that time, it became a new tradition for the Sultans to marry women slaves of the Harem. From that century, the Harem and the Sultanate based upon women slaves. They especially preferred to select Circassian, Georgian and Russian girls in the Harem. Since olden times, the Caucasian girls had been renowned with their beauties in the East. That is why, the Harem received too many Caucasian slaves in the beginning and that number rapidly increased especially in the 17th. Century. The girls taken over as prisoners of war in battlefields used to be taken in the Harem as women slaves earlier but in the decline and regression eras of the Ottomans they lost that source. From then on, The Grand Vizier ,

governors, pashas , governors of provinces and the sisters of the Sultans offered them the women slaves they had raised. Another source was the slaves' having been bought and brought

The slave market in İstanbul by William Allan.

Slave Market, Jean-Lèon Gerome.

in the Harem by the Customs treasurer. In the 19th. Century despite the slavery prohibition in the Empire, Caucasians used to send out their daughters to the Ottoman Harem wishing them to be selected as the wives of the Sultan. And they would even raise their daughters and prepare them for such a life in the Harem by singing them lullabies like 'Hope you will be a wife of the Sultan and lead a glorious life with diamonds'. The women slaves bought outside the Palace at the age of 5-7 used to be raised until they were mature enough, then offered to the Sultan. As they grew bigger and got more beautiful they would take various classes such as music, courtesy, social relations. They used to be taught the ways to treat and serve a man. When they were teenagers, introduced to the initials of the Palace and bought if selected. For the first night, they would stay in the home of the person who had bought them , and if she had some wrong behaviours, physical defects or imperfections noticed that night, then their price would go down and the father be paid less than anticipated. Their parents had to sign a document stating that they sold their daughter and would have no future rights on her. Women slaves accepted in the Harem had to be examined by doctors and midwives. The ones carrying an illness or having some disabilities would never be accepted in the Harem. Extremely beautiful but very inexperienced women slaves were to be trained at first. They would rise to the rank of the assistant-master and the master if they were successful enough. They used to wear long skirts reaching to their heels, tight robes, and coloured chiffon bonnets on their heads. They wore ostentatious robes edged with fringes . As hair care was important to them they would style their hair spending some considerable time in front of mirrors. Some of them used to have such long hair even

Concubines used to wear clothes varying from season to season. Those clothes were tightly stretched on the body and the waist would be tightened by an embellished belt to look slim.

reaching to their heels.

Women slaves were in a kind of competition in the Harem which was like a grand stage set with the players performing in an extravagant costume drama. In order to be noticed they would make-up, tinge their eyes and wear beautiful perfumes. We should mention the pendants, the necklaces and the ear-rings they used to wear too. Those were enhanced with the most precious jewellery such as pearls and diamonds, of course. They always wore seasonal robes. In the summer for instance, you would see them in their light exquisite silk dresses which were rather tight showing off the silhouette of their bodies. Those fur coated dresses had to have laid open collars to bestow a tempting appearance. They had buttons on the front and a rather tightened belt two inches in width enhanced with the most precious jewellery. The belts had buckles amended with diamonds. A cashmere shawl would cover their shoulders. In winters, they would mostly wear fur coats. Women slaves were very well looked after since the Prophet of the Muslims, Mohammed ordered 'Furnish the slaves with anything you eat and wear, and never treat them badly'. The best deed in Islam is granting slaves their liberties. The Prophet Mohammed said 'Whoever grants a Muslim slave his liberty shall not go to hell'. That's why, all the Ottoman Sultans practised this canonical law and gave the unselected women slaves homes prepared their trousseau and let them leave the Harem.

The women slaves completing their training period would compete to become a Master, an Assistant Master, a Gözde (favoured), an İkbal (Sultan's favourite), a Kadın Efendi (Sultan's wife) and finally the Valide Sultana (The Sultana Mother). Women slaves after spending nine years in the Harem had the right to leave. This was called 'Çırağ çıkma'. The Sultan would give

Concubines would be tutored how to read and write along with religious training.

A picture illustrating friendships in the Harem.

her the trousseau and help her marry somebody else. That slave would take a document signed by the Sultan stating her freedom. The woman slave having had that document could do whatever she wanted without any obstructions. Contrary to what is known, the Sultans used to keep 10 to 20 women slaves in their private chambers. The most beautiful ones would be of service to them and the ones who were beautiful enough be sent to the princes' chambers. And finally, the ones who were supposed to become beautiful in the future would be sent to the eunuch treasurer and the assistant masters to be raised.

The young women slaves arriving in the Harem were given different names. Some Persian names such as; Gülnaz, Neşedil, Hoşneva etc. would be given to them according to their behaviours, looks, beauties and characters. To remember their names some rosettes bearing their names would be attached to their collars. Assistant-masters used to train the new comers on Behaviourism, Religion, Sociability, Respectability, Morality and Music if they had the capability. The ones having good voice were given Music classes.

Those women slaves who could rise to the rank of wife had to be meticulously trained by all means and tutored how to read and write. Those women slaves converted to Islam would practise the rules of the religion. They could pray all together or separately. Besides, they were taught how to read the Koran. All women slaves had to be trained on the Islamic religion. After rising to the rank of wife they had many mosques built and charities founded. This shows that they devoted themselves to Islam after having been converted. The letters they wrote are the indicators of their unique training. Along with Music, they were taught poetry and

The concubines received in the Harem would be involved in music apart from the imperial traditions. The miniature made by Levni bears those musician concubines.

literature. Hürrem Sultana made Sultan Süleyman, the Magnificent fall in love with her by sending him the poems she had written. In one of her poems dedicated to Sultan Süleyman she wrote 'Let Hürrem be sacrificed to a single hair of your moustache' (The meaning of these metaphorical lines is 'I wouldn't hesitate to die for you') .

The number of women slaves in the Harem started to increase considerably from the time of Sultan Mehmed, the Conqueror and this number varied during the period of every single Sultan. In Ahmed I.'s period, they changed the heritage system and gave up appointing the Princes to provinces as governors. Instead, they started to accommodate them in the Harem which caused its population rise rapidly, of course. There used to be 300-500 people in the Harem before Mehmed III., but it is known that the number rose to 700 during his period. Women slaves used to be given some per diem the amount of which varied from Sultan to Sultan. For instance, during the period of Mahmud I that amount rose to 30-50 Akçe (Ottoman coins). Money and presents would also be given to them at weddings, festivals, birthdays. While they were taken good care in the Harem , the Sultan was totally intolerant to those who had committed a crime and they used to be exiled to Bursa and the island of Chios. Today, we have a document dated back to 1764 proving that Mustafa III exiled two women slaves to Bursa and Chios. Apart from those of 10-20 women

slaves who were of service to the Sultan directly, the other ones used undertake various posts in the Harem. Inexperienced women slaves would go through a training period at first, with the arrival of the new comers, the existing experienced slaves would promote to the rank of an assistant-master and work in Kadınefendi,

Dancing was as important as music in the Harem. The miniature made by Levni bears the dancing concubine in details.

Valide Sultan, Prince and Gözde chambers. They were classified as the grand, standard and lower assistant masters and worked under the command of the head assistant master in those chambers. 10-15 assistants under the command of the most experienced assistant master would be on duty at night to provide the security of the Harem. Hünkar's (The Sultan) assistant-masters had the most important place in the Harem serving the Sultan in all ways from his bed time arrangement to the preparation of his meals. Those who used to do the Sultan's private and special work were called Hazinedar (Treasurer) and the person managing them, the treasurer master. They used to ranked as 1st., 2nd., 3rd., 4th., and 5th. Hazinedars and remain in the Sultan's chamber whenever the Sultan himself was in the palace. But, only the Hazinedar master could sit by the Sultan as the others were let in when they were called. The 3rd., 4th., and the 5th. Hazinedars used to stand on duty with their assistants outside the Sultan's door for 24 hours. Besides, the key to the treasury was with the Head Hazinedar (The Treasurer). Hazinedars who used to carry the Sultan's seal on a golden pendant around their neck were their confidential friends, too. That is why, the Sultans would always select their own Treasurers and the former ones would either be sent back to the old palace or he let them free by signing of their documentation of freedom. One of the most important duties of the treasurer was to arrange the nights the Kadınefendis would spend with the Sultan. Kethüda Kadın ranking after Kadınefendis was the master of ceremonies which would take place in the Harem. On some important days such as festivals and weddings they used to organise the ceremonies in the Harem. She

would carry a silver rod to express the greatness of her post and used to keep the Sultan's seal to seal his properties in his chamber. Kethüda Kadın had maids help her in everything she did. Çaşnigir Usta (flavour taster) used to deal with all the meals in the Harem. With the women slaves under their control they had to taste all the food the Sultan would eat to find out if anything was poisoned. Çamaşır Usta (Laundry woman) was responsible for the laundry. With the women slaves under their command they always tried to do their best. İbriktar Usta (butler-keeping the ewers) helped the Sultan perform an ablution by pouring water on his hands. Coffee business was Kahveci Usta's and cellar was of Kilerci Usta's duties. Kutucu Usta would wash the Sultans, Kadınefendis and İkbals in the Hamam (Turkish Bath). Külhancı Usta was responsible for the warmth of the Hamams , they had to burn woods to heat the Hamam cabins. A total of 5 Katibe Ustas were in charge of the discipline, regulation and the protocol affairs. The Ustas (masters) examining the sick women slaves used to be called Hastalar Ustası (The master of patients), midwife, and nurses used to work under the control of Kethüda Hanım.

In a list showing the employees of the Harem at the time of Mahmud I, we can see 17 women slaves working in the cellar, 23 under the command of the higher ranked women slaves, 72 for the princes, 15 for İkbals, and 230 various, making a total 456 women slaves. This list proves that The Sultans were not in relation with all Cariyes (women slaves) in the Harem. Hundreds of women slaves coming to the Harem with the hopes of being the Sultan's wife used to be accommodated in the Cariyeler Koğuşu (The chamber of women slaves) to the west of the Harem. They would eat their meals altogether served on big trays directly from the Harem's kitchen by sitting on the bank where the Harem's security guards stood. In the winter time, younger Concubines used to sleep in woolen beds on wooden divans placed on the ground floor of the Concubines chamber which used to be heated by a huge fireplace and have mezzanine floors supported by strong pillars. On top floors, there lived higher ranked Concubines. Inexperienced Concubines were to be inspected by Concubines and them by assistant masters, and finally assistant masters by their masters. They all had a regular life in the Harem.

The gate opening into the Concubines garden bears some scripts revealing the hopes and the dreams of them 'My God who can open all the doors, please open us blessed doors, too). This reflects their common wish and hopes of the future. They all had new dreams everyday and waiting for the day the Sultan would select them.

She was extravagantly beautiful, would display the silhouette of her body under her elaborate tight dress . She would spend a lot of time in front of mirrors watching herself for hours while combing her hair reaching to the ground. She had dimples on her smiling face and was sure of herself that she was admired by all. With her rosy cheeks and vigorous breasts she would stand up and walk into her colourful dreams. Weren't they the same Sultans who had

promoted Hürrem, Safiye, Nakşidil Sultanas to the rank of Sultana from slavery? Sometimes this dream would never come true and their hopes would remain to the following days.

After the period of Ahmed I, Ottoman

The passage from the bath of the Harem to the cold section. C. Rogier. (Library at the Topkapı Palace)

Princes were not appointed to the provinces as governors and they started to stay in the Harem. At times, they had some intercourse with Concubines but since it was prohibited to have children from them they had to comply with the rules. If accidentally one of the Concubines got pregnant she had to lose the baby by mandatory abortion.

It is known that if those voluptuous Concubines were unable to make themselves some room in the Princes chambers either, they used to make love to each other. They would make love with Harem Ağaları (Eunuchs) too, although they were castrated. It is widely known that Eunuchs had many adventures with women slaves. After they were freed and married other people outside the Palace some would divorce a while later saying to the husband 'I used to get more pleasure from my previous intercourse with the black men' is a proof of their adventures with them. We know that Eunuchs would kill each other because of jealousy. Süleyman II reigned between 1687-1691 was sick all the time and had to spend most of his time in Edirne Palace. Making use of his absence, Concubines used to have more relations with Eunuchs. Ahmed II who was living in the Harem as the successor at that time, learnt that from some other Concubines, and after sitting on the throne upon his father's death, banned Eunuchs enter in the Harem after dusk.

At times, those extravagantly beautiful Concubines fell in love with their Music teachers. Kalfa(Assistant Master) used to stand next to them while being tutored. But, their eyes would reveal their desires before words. No words needed in such a case. Hacı Arif Bey, Aziz Efendi, and Sadullah Ağa were some of those who fell in love with their students while tutoring. Hacı Arif Bey was extremely handsome

An engraving illustrating a concubine being tutored under the supervision of a eunuch, belongs to Thomas Allom.

, and the most famous composer of the period. The Sultan was very fond of his work and he had asked him to tutor the Concubines in the Harem. As the classes started their significant glances became more meaningful. He used to make her memorise new songs and would reply back by singing some purposeful songs. That women slave was deeply in love with Hacı Arif Bey, but before she revealed her love to him she had died of tuberculosis. Some other Concubine was clever enough by using the power of the words along with glances and had him love herself. Making love with Concubines was a crime. With the help of some matchmakers, the Sultan allowed his Concubine to marry Hacı Arif Bey.

Aziz Efendi was not so handsome as Hacı Arif Bey, but he had an incredibly beautiful voice. He also taught Concubines in the training room of the Palace. He was too sensitive and quite shy . He could not look at the faces of the Concubines he was tutoring. One day some brought him a Cariye belonged to Hanım Sultana and asked him to train her. She was extremely talented. She could sing the songs perfectly the day after she had learnt them. Aziz Efendi was very much impressed by her ability and took a look at the Concubine admiringly. Their eyes met revealing each other what they had in their hearts. That continued repeatedly every single day, with no words being performed by either. They started to pronounce their love by meaningful songs. But, some day they found out that their classes had been cancelled. Thus, they had to bury their platonic love deep in their hearts. Sometimes such a love would end up in front of an executioner. Sadullah Ağa was one of those who had fallen in love with his student Mihriban and was able to save his head by some piece of music he composed . We are going to tell about his story while narrating Selim III.

Concubines would play some instruments according to their skills. A concubine playing the tambourine.

The Favourites

Extraordinarily beautiful women slaves raised by the Master Treasurer used to be congregated in a separate group named Sultan's assistant masters. The ones the Sultan liked were deposited as odalisques (Majesty's Chamber). The Sultan would select four of them as peyk (for his service) and the other four as Gözde (Favourite). If one of those Gözdes got pregnant she would promote to the rank of İkbal (Felicity) and become Kadın Efendi (Wife). The Sultan would marry the Concubines he did not like, to some other men outside the Harem. There was not a precise rule for the Sultan to keep four Peyks and four Gözdes. It is known that some Sultans used to have fewer women.

The sexual relations of the Sultans with their Concubines have always been told mixing with fantasies by some western authors.

The Venetian envoy Ottoviano Bon (1606), Madam Monteque (1717) and some other travellers furnished us with details of the intimate lives of the Sultans. What O. Bon said, especially copied by other European authors. According to Bon, If the Sultan wanted to see Concubines sing, dance he would whisper the names in Başkadın's ear (Headwoman) who would later send them to the Sultan to be selected. If he liked one of them, then he would walk past them a couple of times giving his handkerchief at the one he liked to spend the

A concubine in the Harem, Jean-Baptiste Hilair.

A Sultan and his favourite, E. Jeaurat.

A favourite. Jean-Auguste Ingres.

Nakşidil Sultana, a favourite of Abdülhamid later promoted to the rank of the Sultana Mother. Painting belongs to Jean-Baptiste Hilair.

night with. Another legend is that, the Sultan threw a handkerchief at the girl he liked who was to take and put it in her bosom. Another way was that the woman slave selected and raised by the Treasurer Master and accommodated with Kahveci Usta (Coffee Maker) would serve the Sultan coffee with the hope of being selected. If the Sultan liked that Concubine he would take her into his private Odalisques. The Sultan would send some gifts to the one he intended to spend the night with. Then, the selected Concubine would be escorted to the Hamam (The Bath) soaped and scrubbed raw with the spongelike tropical gourd, and ladled perfumed water over one another. After the bath, they used to be put in loose, clean garments. She would be escorted into the Sultan's chamber (Odalisques) by the Master Treasurer. In the chamber, she had to wait outside until the Sultan went into bed. When she entered the room she would crawl towards the bed and after reaching, she would stand up and go into his bed. But, Madam Monteque wrote that, as she had been told by Mustafa I.'s İkbal, Hafsa Sultan, the handkerchief throwing and crawling were all made up stories.

The following morning, the Sultan would take a bath in the Sultan's Hamam, change his clothes and send the Concubine he had spent the night with some presents, jewellery and clothes if he had found the night satisfactory. That Concubine would reach to the rank of Gözde then. She was escorted back and given a separate chamber with slaves under her command. The following legend furnishing us with details on how to become a Gözde favourite is quite interesting.

Aimee de Rivery born in 1763 in the island of Martinique, was the daughter of a very noble family and the cousin to Josephine Bonaparte, Napoleon's wife. As they were being raised together in their childhood a fortune-teller came up one day saying to the two girls 'You, Josephine! you are going to be the Queen of France in the future , and you, little Aimee! you are going to be the Queen of a country in the East in the future.' They wondered if that would come true. In 1784, on her return to Martinique, after attending convent school in France, Aimee was kidnapped by Algerian pirates . Twenty-one years old, Aimee was sold to the Dey of Algiers. Captivated by her beauty, the Dey saw an opportunity to win the Sultan's favour. He presented the girl to Abdulhamid I. She was fair, demure and intelligent. The Sultan named her Nakşidil (Embroidered on the Heart), converted her to Islam and made her his favourite as odalisques.

In Michel De Grece's book 'La nuit du Serail', the presentation of Nakşidil Sultana's to the Sultan is described as follows;

"First, I was escorted to Valide Sultana's Hamam. I was soaped, scrubbed raw and given a perfect massage with some oil. Then, they brushed my long hair down my back. They sprayed perfumes with different odours in Bohemian crystal bottles on all parts of my body. After that, the master of the robes brought me a white blouse, almost transparent, embroidered with silver stripes lightly, a pair of red satin baggy trousers and a dress enhanced

Sultan Abdülhamid I pictured in this painting by Jean-Baptiste Hilair.

with silver stripes in flower patterns. They wound a purple girdle made of Persian brocade around my ostentatious waist. The final stage was the jewellery clerk's business. She brought in her small chest of drawers filled up with jewels. She took out a very long pendant enhanced with ruby repoussé golden rings. Two big pearls were my ear-rings. They put a pink net-lace on my hair amended with rubies and diamonds. I was ready. I got scared to death... Vartuhi instructed me what I was supposed to do one by one: "About half an hour later His Majesty will be in his chamber. Then, you will be escorted to him. Don't you ever forget to walk to his bed on your knees, and to kiss his bedcover by holding it on the edge and to wait." "...Kızlarağası (Chief-footman) appeared in the splendour of his red silk clothing with sable fur. Eunuchs were following him. They were coming to escort me to the Sultan's chamber..." With a confident voice, I said " I am ready".

The harem women by A. de Favray.

All the lights along the corridors and the courtyard were dimmed and the Harem as I was walking behind the Chief-footman was getting ready for the night. We walked past the chambers of Valide Sultana and the long, dark and empty corridor of the Sultan's Hamam. As we arrived right outside that huge gate, the Chief-footman bowing in front of me , kissed the hem of my dress and showed me the way in. I walked into Abdülhamid's bedroom in twilight. I stood right by the door for a short time watching the bright, splendid ceiling. Two old ladies were sitting still on the floor quietly. No doubt, they were the women in charge of the illumination of the chamber.

"Come by girl, don't be afraid!" I was unable to see the man calling me with a sweet voice. I made a step, then the second one. Despite the instructions of Vartuhi, I walked towards the Sultan's bed without kneeling down. With a movement of his hand, I was seated by the edge of his embroidered bed with cushions on. He was glancing at me very comfortably. And me, without blinking, glanced back at him. In his long navy shirt, the Sultan was unimpressive without diamonds and his turban. He was almost bald. He suddenly started to recite an ode from the poet Nedim "My beautiful lady who brought you up fearlessly" As he finished, without taking his eyes off he came next to me. Very slowly, he began caressing my breasts on the transparent fabric which was covering my head, shoulders and arms. Continuously, he was whispering some lovely words into my ear. His voice and its tune amazed me. I felt my body in an unresisting numbness and started to feel some hotness deep inside my bosom. When he started to undress me very slowly I deliberately let him kiss all parts of my body. I soon, found myself as a rosy-tanned naked blonde lying on the dark-coloured velvet. I suddenly startled with the awareness of those two old ladies sitting on the ground. But, he had already begun spreading my legs wide-open with his soft and determined hands. At that very moment, I got totally oblivious of all my embarrassment. Some passion pushed me hard towards that man. As I was only feeling the warmth and the weight of that body on mine , I let myself in the waves.

While we were resting together side by side after our passion died down, I suddenly felt some shivers deep inside me accompanied by a muscular shock on my hand."

"When I woke up, I found myself alone in the room. Through the high and small windows of the room some disturbing sun light was shining on the extravagant decoration of the wooden veneers and the bedstead... A cobalt-blue fur coat was sitting at the foot of the bedstead undercoated with silver chinchilla. On his pillow, there was a large purse by a rounded bright red ruby enhanced with a diamond. The presents Abdülhamid left for me...

I had just sat up when the door opened. Beside the Chief-footman, eunuchs who had been waiting to watch me wake up entered in. They put the fur coat on me in a little hasty but a respectful manner..."

So, after a night spent in the Sultan's bed I rose to the rank of İkbal... Nakşidil Sultana rising to the rank of İkbal, gave birth to a baby son named Mahmud and deserved the rank of the fourth Kadınefendi (Sultan's wife). In the meantime, she learnt a lot about the intrigues and contentions when the first Kadınefendi Nükhetseza and the second Mihrişah Sultana had a fierce struggle to have their own sons sit on the throne.

In 1789, when the French Revolution had already started, Abdülhamid died. Selim III, Mihrişah Sultana's son sat on the Ottoman throne. He wanted Nakşidil Sultana to stay in the Harem with his son since he really got on well and shared his secrets with her. Nakşidil Sultana was a part of the French culture he deeply admired. She was teaching the Sultan French and had already become the pioneer of the reforms taking place in the Palace. Selim III.'s radical movement made the bigots angry. They rebelled in 1807 and killed almost all the members of the Sultan's family but Nakşidil Sultanas' son Mahmud II. He sat on the throne, and thus, Nakşidil Sultana became Valide Sultana (The Sultana Mother). Having been brought up by her mother with a Western culture he started reforms. His strongest supporter was his mother of course.

Until her early death in 1817, Nakşidil Sultana remained as Valide Sultana. She died young and buried in a sepulchre mentioned by her name in Fatih. Nakşidil Sultana went into the Harem as a French girl, had lot of public fountains and charity foundations built. As an unforgettable Valide Sultana she has a historical importance.

The harem women by A. de Favray.

Felicities

If the women slaves taken in the Harem to be raised for the Sultan's private chamber got pregnant, then, they would be called İkbals (felicities), If the number of İkbals the Sultan had was more than one then they would be named as the Head İkbal, the second, the third and the fourth. When one of them gave birth she would rise to the rank of Kadın Efendi (Sultan's Wife). But, that tradition was not always practised. For instance, Mahmud II.'s İkbal, Pertevniyal Sultana was promoted to the rank of the Sultan's wife right after the birth of her baby. But, Sultan Abdülmecid's head İkbal Nalandil was never given the rank of the Sultan's wife although she gave birth.

İkbal class started in the period of Mustafa II. The name of the first İkbal was Fatma Şahin Hanım. Later, Ahmed III had one, Mahmud I four, Mustafa III one, Selim III one, Mahmud II four, Abdülmecid six, and Abdülhamid four İkbals. İkbals became more important by the end of the 18th. century and were some of the most significant women in the Harem in the 19th. century. İkbals and Kadın Efendis were able to keep their present status even after the Sultan's death.

Sultans loved some of their İkbals more than Kadın Efendis (their wives). For example, Abdülhamid II loved his head İkbal Müşfika Kadın too much and honoured her with the rank of Kadın Efendi later. İkbals used to stay in the Gözde-İkbal chamber Abdülhamid I had it built. They had slaves serving them.

The painting by Frederich Arthur Bridgman "The Favourites and the Felicities".

The painting by Emanuel de Dieudonne "Odalisques", private collection.

49

Each İkbal had a private room with a fireplace and enameled closets on the top floor of Gözde's chamber right next to the Princes' one in the courtyard. That was built by the order of Abdülhamid I. Those rooms overlooking the Golden Horn had separate toilets and Hamams too. Their maids' rooms which were much smaller were on the ground floor. On the upper floor, there was a large hall where Haseki Sultans lived and the İkbals gathered to chat at times. The concealed passage between that chamber and the reception hall connecting the Sultans to the İkbals directly was a revolution in the Palace. The Sultans' daughters, princes, Kadın Efendis and İkbals were supplied with clothing, food and firewood everyday. Besides, the women and the princes would get their daily food in 15 dishes the menu of which was chicken and meat most of the time. They were also served clotted cream, stewed fruit, butter, yoghurt and fruits everyday. Those were only given to the ones who had chambers in the Palace. The others would have different foods. Princes, Kadın Efendis and İkbals would get some snow to cool their drinks in the summer time.

The Sultans Wives

The women of the Ottoman Sultans' used to be called Kadın Efendiler (Sultan's wife). The number of Kadın Efendis would vary from four to eight. The first wife was called the Head Wife, the others respectively; the second, third, fourth and so on. They used to stay in their private chambers with their slaves and assistant masters. Upon one's death, one of the İkbals would rise to the rank of Kadın Efendi. The Chief-footman had to present the Sultan with the promotion of an İkbal to the rank of Kadın Efendi. The Sultan had to approve of that promotion himself. After his approval, Kadın Efendi was to be given a letters-patent, and new dresses had to be ordered for her. Then, she was given a separate chamber. She would also be trained by Hazinedar Usta (Treasurer) and his assistants on Imperial traditions. Kadın Efendis who had children between 16th. and 18th. centuries were named Haseki Sultan. This title was first given to Sultan Süleyman, the Magnificent's wife Hürrem Sultana.

The first, second and the third Kadın Efendis had their own chambers in the Cariyes' courtyard of the Palace. Kadın Efendis would be with the Sultan in those chambers ornamented with fireplaces, in turns. They had the stick to their rotation. The Sultans had the right to spend the nights with anybody they would like to but Friday nights they had to be with their own wives. This was an Islamic order. If a wife wasn't with her husband for three consecutive Fridays, they had

The armorial bearing is beautifully pictured in the painting by John Frederic Lewis "The Life in the Harem".

Haseki Sultana and her assistant.

the right to go to the Kadı (Ottoman Judge). Their rotation would be arranged by the Hazinedar Usta (The Treasurer). Once, Gülfem Sultana who was in need of money for the mosque she was having built, sold her turn to another woman and unfortunately got killed by the order of Sultan Süleyman who said the incident was an insult to the Sultan himself.

Hazinedar Usta, as he used to fix the wives' rotation, would also arrange some other wives for the Sultan. For instance, He arranged the sixth wife of Mahmud I and the third wife of Abdülhamid I, Nevres Kadın as the third Kadın Efendi.

Earlier, Kadın Efendis used to live with the Princes in Provinces but later as the Princes were called back at the Harem for good they had to stay in the Kadın Efendis' chambers until they died or the Sultan left the throne. But if the Sultans were dethroned, they would then be sent to the old Palace and the new Sultans would replace them in their own chambers.

Although they were with the Sultan by rotation, nobody should expect the Sultan to love all of them equally. Some Harem rumours revealed that some of them were really adored and some neglected. For instance, Sultan Süleyman, the Magnificent first married Mahidevran, but later he fell in love with Hürrem and started spoiling her. Those two women had a long-lasting row. And, one day Mahidevran beat Hürrem in the Harem. When Sultan Süleyman learnt about the incident he immediately ordered her to be sent to Manisa where her son had been

The happiness of a favourite or a felicity after giving birth and promoted to the rank of the wife of the Sultan pictured in the painting by Frederick Goodall "A new light in the Harem".

living.

Another incident was between Avcı Mehmed's first wife Gülnuş Sultana and Cariye Gülbeyaz. When the Sultan preferred the new Cariye Gülbeyaz to his first wife, she could not endure as she loved him too much and killed Gülnuş Sultana by throwing her off the rocks when all the Cariyes were having a picnic by the seaside. Thus, she was able to get rid of her rival. We know that some Kadın Efendis as much effective on the Sultans as they would intervene the Imperial affairs. It is recorded that some of those even ruled the Empire by introducing their own Imperial policies. In the Ottoman Empire, that era was called 'The Women's Sultanate'. This topic will be told in Valide Sultans' section.

Kadın Efendis used to wear overcoats in Summers and fur coats in the wintertime. As they went by the Sultan's side they would take their coat off and give it to the Assistant Concubine. They had to stand until the Sultan let them to sit. The one in front of them was the only magistrate of the Ottoman Empire and the Caliph of the Islam at the same time. So, without his permission, the women would neither talk nor behave informally. Kadın Efendis used to call their sons 'His Majesty', and when they came to visit them, they would stand up and meet them saying 'My brave young man!'. Regardless of their ages, the Princes would kiss the Kadın Efendis' hand as a sign of respect. The other women in the

Coffee serving in the Harem.

The concubines in the painting of Jean-Baptiste Hilair, Gallery Mathaf, London.

Harem, to show their respect, would kiss, Kadın Efendi's skirt. When one Kadın efendi wanted to speak to another, she would send out her own messenger to ask for her convenience. They were quite formal to one another. When they had to go out, they would take their own Concubines and the assistants with them.

A Harem Ağası (Eunuch) would escort their cart on foot. If all Kadın Efendis set off altogether, then their carts would go in a row according to their seniority.

The most important thing to the women of the Harem was their hair. As Concubines, Kadın Efendis were very fond of their hair care, they would spend hours in front of mirrors. If they had long hair, one's plaiting it would take hours. On their plaited hair they used to wear some precious ribbons and pins. When they wore a bonnet, their hair would be hidden in it. The bonnets they wore on their head were a little lopsided. Their bonnets were made of velvet enhanced with pearls and diamonds for the winter. And, for the summer they used to have bonnets made of very light fabric enhanced with either an attached rose with a diamond or a golden pin on an embroidered handkerchief. Most of the time, they would attach a flower and an aigrette made of precious stones on their bonnets. Those aigrettes were both very precious and embroidered very elegantly at the same time.

The Daughters of The Sultans

The children of the Ottoman Sultans were called; Sultanas if they were their daughters, and Şehzade (Prince) if they were the sons. The daughters were given names such as Ayşe, Fatma and Emine, and called Ayşe Sultana, Fatma Sultana etc.

People in the Harem would experience a great fuss if one of the İkbals or Hanım Sultanas got pregnant. The Sultana Mother would talk to his son to start the preparations for the expected baby. Then, she would talk to the Treasurer Official to raise some money and obtain the provisions. One of the birth rooms of the Harem would be prepared for the forthcoming birth and redecorated. The birth room had splendid material enhanced with pearls and diamonds. The cradles, curtains and the bed linens used to be made of the most precious fabric. A mosquito-net would be placed above the bed having made from red satin which was the favourite colour of the Ottomans, enhanced with pearls, rubies and emeralds. All the material brought in the birth room would be registered in a book. The Harem used to have quite a few cradles permanently since they experienced a few births a week or a month. From time to time, the golden cradle which is exhibited today in the Ottomans' Treasury would be brought in from the birth room to be utilised for some births. Those cradles would be covered in the most precious embroidered fabric and enhanced with precious stones. They would have a nazarlık set (amulet worn against the evil eye), a small Koran case and an inscription of the word Maşaalah (God save him!) enhanced with diamonds, rubies and brilliants. The Sultan would give the mother and the midwife a lot of presents after the baby was born. If that was her first baby, then the number of presents was likely to be more.

Soon after the baby was born, Harem Ağası (Eunuch) was the first to learn about the birth. He would send out the birth room master to let

The cradle used for the babies of the Sultans.

A Koran case had to be in the room where the cradle was placed.

Silahtar Ağa (Esquire of the Sultan) know about the good news and announce it to the Palace. All the members of the gynecium (Ladies rooms) had to kill rams for celebration. The number of rams to be killed by the members of every single chamber would be five if the baby was a boy and three if it was a girl. Seven cannon balls would be fired from the palace if the baby was a boy, and three if it was a girl. They would fire five times a day at intervals to let the public know about the good news. At the same time, the public messengers would roam about the streets of the Empire calling out 'the Sultan had a baby'.

The birth of the baby would be announced outside Istanbul and at the remote parts of the Empire by the Grand Vizier through the Sultan's firman (Decree of the Sultan). The Grand Vizier would come to the Palace the following day with the members of the chancery for congratulation. After the congratulation ceremony sherbet (diluted fruit juices) would be served. It was a tradition to serve the Sultan sherbet on the third day following the birth. Sherbet would also be served to those who came to visit the baby. Those sherbets would be served by beautiful Concubines in golden and silver mugs. The Harem would welcome the birth of the baby in great enthusiasm.

The cradle and its cover enhanced with precious stones of the recently born Sultan would be brought in the Palace with ceremonies. Those precious materials The Sultana Mother had prepared used to be kept in the old palace until

An Ottoman Grand Vizier.

the birth. After the birth they would be brought in Topkapı Palace by the chief-footman with ceremonies. That was called The Sultana Mother cradle procession. When the procession started the chief-footman would deliver the cradle to the Sultan's Kethüda (Official for Home Affairs) with ceremonies. That official would deliver the cradle to the Sultana Mother's Kahvecibaşı (Head coffee maker) and its quilt to his assistant. Those coffee makers would receive those by raising them to the top of their heads and so , the ceremony would start. And, the public gathering by the sides of the road to the new Palace would applaud wishing the new Sultan a long life. The Chief-footmen getting off their horses would line up in two rows and walking through the middle gate, made their way towards the gate of the Harem by the chancery of the Palace in the third courtyard. The head coffee makers would deliver the cradle, its cover and the quilt to The Sultana Mother's chief-footman. The chief-footman, by kissing and rising the stuff on top his head would deliver them to the Harem Ağası (Eunuch) with ceremonies. The Eunuch, accompanied by other eunuchs would take all the property into the Harem and deliver them to the women who were in charge of that business. The Eunuch then, would come back to hand out the monies the Sultan had given him to distribute to the ones who attended the ceremony.

Apart from that, there used to be another cradle procession organised by the Grand Vizier leaving the Sultana Mother's ceremony in the shade. It was more crowded and splendid. The ceremony that had to take place on the sixth day following the birth was for the Imperial officials to visit the new mother. Her mother would also attend the ceremony to see her daughter on that day, too.

The Grand Vizier would have a cradle, a quilt and a cradle cover enhanced with precious stones soon after the baby was born. If the baby was a boy then an aigrette enhanced with precious stones would be added on top of that.

On the fifth day following the birth, invitation cards would be sent to the ones who would attend the ceremony by the Grand Vizier's official and they would be asked to gather outside the pasha gate at the required time. The following day, the ceremony would start outside the pasha gate where the guests were already ready. In that ceremony, the Grand Vizier would deliver his presents to Kethüda Bey (Official responsible for home affairs). Those, after placing the presents on their heads, would start the procession in the harmony of the marches played by Mehter Takımı (the Ottoman Military Band). Since there used to be so many different people attending the ceremony, the colours of their clothes would create a multicoloured scene on the procession ground. There used to be so many officials on the ground such as; Kılavuz Çavuş (The Sergeant Guide), the Imperial Chancery Sergeants, The Grand Vizier, the Chief-Footman of the Gynecium, the Sergeants Clerk, and foot equerries. That cradle procession the Grand Vizier organised would last for days. The parade would reach Bab-ı Hümayun (The Imperial gate) along Divan yolu, having been headed towards the Harem through the middle gate. The Chief-Footman would take the cradle, its cover and the quilt, and donate the attendants with fur coats, clothes, fabric and monies according to their ranks. The Eunuch would take the cradle to the Sultan for his inspection. After being inspected by the Sultan, the cradle would be sent to the new mother's room. The room would be filled up with many visitors, like The Sultana Mother, the other wives of the Sultan, The Sultan's favourites, standing in a row according to their ranks. The Sultana Mother would be seated on a higher ground surrounded by the people of her blood.

The other visitors would be seated on the cushions placed on wooden banks and wait for the cradle the Sultan was to send. Finally, the cradle would arrive in the room. They all were to stand up to salute the cradle. When the cradle set arrived in the middle of the room, the Sultana Mother would throw a handful of golden liras into it followed by the others. After that, the midwife would lay the child in the new cradle by saying some prayers. She would then rock it for three times. All the presents the visitors brought would be left on the cradle. Actually, those presents were for the midwife, that's why, she would take them after the ceremony.

The women visitors would give presents to the baby and its mother according to the rank of their husbands. Those presents would be shown to the Sultan and registered in the accounts book.

An Ottoman Prince.

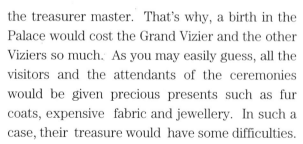

The caftan (95 cms.) of the daughter of Mustafa III (1757-1774), Fatma Sultana.

The gold-embroidered caftan of Saliha Sultana which she wore in her childhood, 72 cms.

The women visitors used to be hosted in the Harem for three days and would take part in the entertainment organised by the Concubines. They would listen to the saz (stringed instrument) played by them, the songs they sang and watched gypsy dancers. It was traditional for those women visitors to deliver presents not only for the mother and the baby but also the daughters and the sons of the Sultan as well as the treasurer master. That's why, a birth in the Palace would cost the Grand Vizier and the other Viziers so much. As you may easily guess, all the visitors and the attendants of the ceremonies would be given precious presents such as fur coats, expensive fabric and jewellery. In such a case, their treasure would have some difficulties.

The recently born babies would be donated with a new chamber in the Harem. They would have maids, women slaves and wet nurses. Beside the mother, their maids and the assistant masters would help the baby grow too. The daughters of the Sultan would play with the children of their age in the Palace and when it was time to start their education, some teachers would be selected to tutor them. As they were starting their education, the Sultan would start his child's education by saying the first Besmele (Meaning 'In God's Name'). Then, he would give the child an alphabet book and a Koran.

Besides, he would furnish the child with a velvet book case the cover of which was enhanced with pearl and silver embroidery. The cover would also bear the Imperial emblem.

The classes in the Harem would take place in the Princes' study room on top of the chamber belonging to Darüssade Ağası (The Head Eunuch). The major lesson was 'Reading the Koran properly' followed by Reading and Writing, Maths, History and Geography. In the 19th. Century, French and piano classes were added. The daughter of the Sultan having completed her education would wear long dresses and cover her

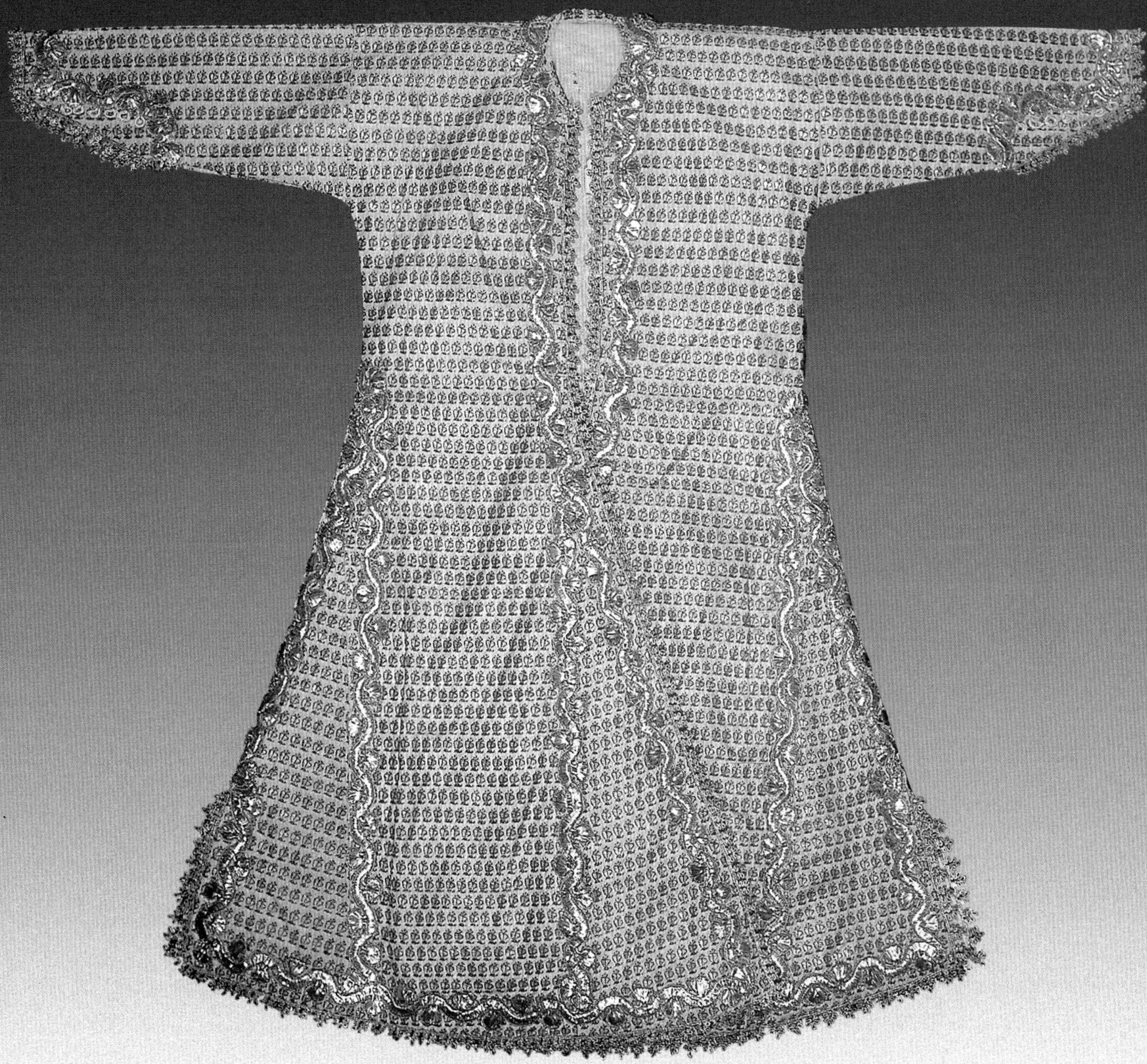

hair with a yashmak (formerly worn by Turkish women). When they reached the age appropriate for the marriage at that time , they would be married to the Princes of the neighbouring Principalities. But, when the Principalities collapsed, they started to get married to the viziers, pashas and the Imperial officials. When the Sultan wanted to marry his sister or daughter to one of those, he would order the Grand Vizier to find an appropriate candidate for them. Once the candidate was selected he had to send in the engagement set to the Palace. If the candidate selected by the Grand Vizier was married, he was forced to divorce. Sokollu Mehmed Pasha was one of them as he was forced to divorce his two wives. The famous Grand Vizier, Nevşehirli İbrahim Pasha had to divorce his wife when he was selected as the candidate. The Sultans had the right to select the candidate in their daughters' names. Their daughters had to obey their fathers. Since the candidates were senior officials in the Empire, they were of course, at an old age when they got married. That's why, they would die a little after the marriage, leaving young widows behind. The lives of those old bridegrooms were not so colourful. The first step they would make was to divorce their wives. They had no rights to remarry or divorce the Sultans' daughters even if they did not like them. They also, had to forget all about the Concubines. Besides, they would never go on their own. They had to obey the Sultans by all means, and could not even sit down without the Majesty's permission. As they were unable to

divorce their wives, on the contrary, their wives could divorce them with the permission of the Majesties.

If the Sultan got angry with the bridegroom after the marriage, he would dismiss him. For example, the daughter of Yavuz Sultan Selim, Shah Sultan got married The Grand Vizier Lütfi Pasha who was an austere man. Some day, his officers caught a man making love with a prostitute and directly brought them to the Pasha. He ordered the woman to be operated on her vagina. Having heard that, Shah Sultan had a fierce row with him that night. She said to him that, it was brutal and he shouldn't have done so. But, Lütfi Pasha yelled "If they bring me another woman like that, I am going to do the same again." When the Eunuchs heard them have a row they immediately came up and threw him out of the Harem. The following day, when the Sultan heard all about it, dismissed Lütfi Pasha from all his offices including the marriage. Another incident belongs to Murad IV. When Murad IV got angry with his daughter's husband Admiral Hasan Pasha and dismissed him. As it is easily understood, it was not so easy to be a son-in-law in the Palace. Sultanas used to be engaged when they were very young and married at the age of fourteen or fifteen. To empower her sultanate, Kösem Sultana married the Sultan's daughters at very early ages to the pashas of the time, and unfortunately that culture continued for quite a while until Mahmud II. stopped it. He put a limit on that by prohibiting under age marriages.

A miniature of two lovers bearing the men's and the women's clothes of the 16th. century.

A sultana is putting on her clothes, Amedee Van Loo, Louvre Museum, Paris.

The Sultana Weddings

The engagement and wedding ceremonies of the Sultanas would either be on the same day or different. They would be wedded by Şeyh-ül İslam (The head of the Ottoman Muslims). The representative of the bridegroom would be the Grand Vizier or his assistant in his absence, and the Sultanas' the Head Eunuch. He would manage the wedding ceremony, too. The weddings of the Sultanas would take place in the Imperial chancery and the others in the head Eunuch's chamber. The visitors of the Sultan's blood would wear fur coats and hilats (Robe of honour awarded by the Sultan). Besides, the Sultana would send his future husband a hilat. It was the head Eunuch's duty to dress the bridegroom in that hilat.

The Sultana whose father was on the throne would have such a splendid wedding lasting for a week or two. The Sultanas whose fathers were dethroned or died would have less important weddings. When the daughter of Mehmed IV married Musahip Mustafa Pasha in 1675, her wedding lasted for twenty days during which the visitors were all feasted every single day of it. The Sultans would donate the newly wed couple with splendid villas and decorate the interior parts. The trousseau of the bride should have been prepared well beforehand. If there was anything missing then they would add in that, too. There would be an entertainment in the Harem for the bride where people could sing, dance, play instruments etc.. The town would also be embellished with arches, flags and so on. Fireworks would lighten up the streets under the lanterns' pale light. The

Sultans would have mansions built for the newly-wed couple. Hatice Sultana Sabil Mansion is one of those.

67

ententainment would continue in the streets as well. The Sultans would get a lot of money for the wedding from the treasury. They always wanted to arrange glorious wedding ceremonies for their daughters. But, of course, they actually wanted to show off their strength to the public.

Mirrors, the concubines were very much in need of. Some of them are embellished with precious stones. They might have been used by the Sultans' wives.

The trousseau of the bride would be exhibited in the Palace for the public. The Grand Vizier and other officials would send their presents to the Palace too. May be, the brightest part of the wedding was the Kına night(Applying henna to the bride's fingers and toes). That night, the wives of the Viziers, the family of Yeniçeri Ağası (The head of the new Ottoman Army) would be invited for the festivities. The Sultan's wives would host them all during the night. The ladies attending the night would bring in some presents according to the rank of their husbands. The Grand Vizier would keep a book that had to be examined by the Sultan beforehand and write down the names of the other Viziers' wives who would attend the night. He would also add in the list of all the presents to be taken to the bride name by name. The residents of the Harem and the guests would entertain to their hearts' content. Kına (Henna) would be applied in their palms and left there for a day to form a reddish colour. It was a kind of make-up for the women of the time. Today, this tradition still continues in some Anatolian villages. When the Henna night was over the guests would be put up in the Palace so that they could attend the Bride's procession the following day (Thursday). The bride would be escorted to the bridegroom's home in a glorious procession.

The Sultana would go on a horse-drawn red carriage which was an emblem of the Empire. The carriage would be covered by a mosquito net, too. Her being escorted on a twin horse-drawn carriage was an Ottoman tradition. When the Sultana arrived at the bridegroom's home, she would be met by his future husband and the Girls' Footman. They would be escorted to the gate of the Harem. At the bridegroom's home, the male and the female guests would be feasted in separate halls. After the night prayers, they would all leave his home having accepted the presents given by the bridegroom. After that, the Head Eunuch, after dressing the bridegroom in a sable fur and introducing him to the Sultan would leave the place. Later, the bridegroom would be escorted into the room by the bridesmaid. After completing his prayers in a corner of the room, he would kiss the skirt of his wife and stood there until the Sultan let him sit down. That was an indication of the respect shown towards the Sultan and his relatives. The Sultanas would have maids in their splendid mansion appointed by the Sultan himself. All work including shopping was their business. The Sultanas had a good income from their estates donated them by the Sultan. If the daughter of the Sultan gave birth to a baby daughter, then the baby would be called 'Hanım Sultana'. When they grew up and reached at an appropriate age for the marriage, they would be wedded by the Vice Chancellor of Rumeli(Turkish land in Europe). Their sons would be called 'bey'. When they grew up they would be given various posts at the Palace. Their daughters used to have regular salaries paid by the treasury. Without the Sultan's permission they had no right to divorce their husbands either. The Sultan would go to their home and dress the bridegroom in a fur coat. And

so, the ceremony was over. The Sultans who had more than one daughter, had to accomplish the same procedure for all of them. Of course the heavy load was always on the Treasury. As told above, that Ottoman tradition still continues in Anatolia in a modest way.

The corona like a flower bouquet lent by the treasure for the wedding ceremony. It is made of precious stones and has a rose like emerald in the middle.

69

The Princes

Princes were the sons of the Sultans born of their Haseki (Privileged wives), İkbal (Felicities) and Gözde (The favourites) sultanas. As we already told about the birth, cradle ceremonies and celebrations of the Sultans' children, there is no need to repeat that again.

When the Princes reached at the age of five or six, they would start their education with a ceremony in the Princes' School on the upper floor of Darüssade Ağası (The Head Eunuch). The Princes' school built in the 15th. century and restored in the 16th. and 19th. centuries had a classroom right across the vast entrance hall. A large fireplace, bookcases, shelves, lecterns and ceilings with mirrors and vaults were the evidence of its importance. Although the Princes used to be with their mothers and maids until the age of eight, they could only be with their Lalas (Man servants having the care of a child prince) and tutors from that age until they became adults. They could only see their parents on some special occasions.

Their circumcision feasts staged splendid celebrations. Three months before it commenced, all the Viziers, Sultans, Statesmen of all the Ottoman States had been invited for the ceremonies. Those circumcision feasts would continue for ten or fifteen days and sometimes more, of course. In 1457, The Conqueror's sons Bayezıd and Mustafa's circumcision feasts lasted for a month with the participation of the Kings of the neighbouring countries. The preparations for Murad III's son, Prince Mehmed's circumcision

The princes who sat on the throne would go horseback for the feasts and to gird on a sword.

71

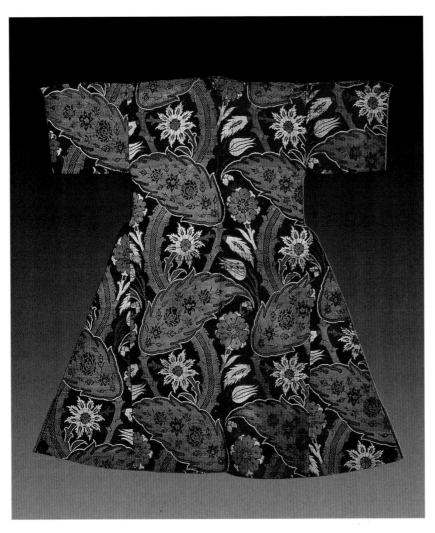

feasts had started one year before it commenced. For that feast, three storey platform was built at The İbrahim Pasha Palace for the Sultan and his guests, large tents were put up at the At(Horse)Square for the banquet and the area was illuminated by oil lamps. For the feast that would last for 52 days, The Kings, Emperors of many countries all over the world were invited. The Imperial officials, senior military officers, Moslem theologians, businessmen and the representatives of foreign countries attended the feasts and brought in their presents according to their social classes. The guests were entertained and feasted all during the ceremonies.

The feasts that had taken place at that At Square were proven with the miniatures made by Nakkaş Osman. Another splendid circumcision feast that we know was for Ahmed III's sons Mehmed, Mustafa III and Bayezıd. That lasted for fifteen days in 1720. Those feasts took place in Okmeydanı and Haliç (The Golden Horn) both on land and on the sea. Poet Vehbi pencilled that feast in. Levni proved the feast with his miniatures that he collected in an album.

The Princes used to have a chamber in the Harem in which they lived until the age of 13 or 14. When the Princes whose fathers were alive had to go out of the Palace, would wear fur coats and aigrettes. Horse riding archery and hunting were their usual outdoor activities. The ones whose fathers were dead, would live in seclusion in their own chambers. Those would be given a house in the large courtyard of the Harem. The room in which they stayed, actually locked up, called 'the cage'. The Princes who were experiencing a secluded life in that cage used to have twelve Concubines(Women Slaves), one footman from the treasury, and another from the cellar.

The throne would be unattended when the Sultan died, withdrew or was dethroned. Murad II left the throne to his son Sultan Mehmed, the Conqueror by his consent. But, Bayezıd II had to leave the throne to his younger son Selim by force. Osman, İbrahim and Mustafa IV were the Sultans who were dethroned and replaced by the other Sultans. Darüs-saade Ağası (The Head Eunuch) would let the Prince know about his father's dead or dismissal. He would hold him by the arm and escort him to show the dead body of his father. The Lifeguard would also hold him by the other arm and take him to Hırka-i Şerif chamber (Mohammed's Cloak-kept in Istanbul). There, while the Grand Vizier and the Head of The Ottoman Muslims, Şeyh-ül İslam were recognising him as a sovereign, the ceremony preparations had already begun. His accession to the throne was immediately announced to the public and the guests would be invited in for the ceremonies.

The throne of the Sultan would be placed right outside the Ak Ağalar gate called Babüs-Saade. The guests would line up according to their ranks in the courtyard. The Sultan, already waiting in the next room, would come and sit on the throne having been escorted by Babüs-saade Ağası(The Felicity Footman) and the Esquire. The guests attending the ceremony would recognise him as a sovereign one by one. And finally the ceremony would end when Şeyh-ül İslam, The Grand Vizier and the other Viziers, waiting under the dome, recognised him as a sovereign. After that, the Sultan would gird on a sword in Eyüp as per traditions. That could correspond to the coronation ceremonies of the European Kings. A few days after he sat on the throne, he would go there either by sea or overland to gird on the sword. That was called the Sultan's procession of girding on the sword after accession.

The Eunuchs

We know that, there used to be Harems in palaces of olden times safeguarded by castrated Eunuchs. For example, as it is recorded in history Assyrian Harem was protected by black Eunuchs. The famous historian Heredotos mentioned about a merchant named Ponyonus from Chios who was in the slavery business. Castration first appeared in Assyrian. Later, it appeared in Iran. And, through Syria and Anotolia, it was conveyed to Greece and Italy. It is known that the Artemis Temple in Ephesus which is one of the seven wonders of the world was safeguarded by castrated monks named 'Sibel'.

In the Medieval age, black Eunuchs existed in the Abbaside and Mameluke palaces got conveyed to the Ottomans. They were mostly sent to the Ottomans by the governors of Egypt. All throughout the Ottoman period they were always responsible for the Harem. As the Grand Vizier İbşir Mustafa Pasha wanted to keep them away from the Palace once, he was unable to do so. At the time of Ahmed III, the Grand Vizier Şehit Ali Pasha ordered the Governor of Egypt to castrate all the Abyssinians in Egypt. But, it was never practised upon his death. We know that their existence in the Ottoman Harem started at the time of Sultan Mehmed the Conqueror and their importance grew from the period of Beyazid II. As the Harem was previously called 'Darüssaade', they were named as

A painting by Van Mour, a eunuch and his master are illustrated.

A eunuch safeguarding the Harem.

'Darüsssaade Ağası'. Later, they used to be called 'Harem Ağası' or 'Kızlar Ağası'(Eunuch). While the black Eunuchs protected the Palace, the white ones protected Babüssaade(The middle gate). That gate opening into Enderun (Gynecium/Ladies apartments) was therefore called Ak Ağalar Kapısı (White Eunuch Gate). The Harem used to be protected by the White Eunuchs at first, but Murad III appointed Abyssinian Mehmed Ağa as the Eunuch in 1582. And since then, they were all selected amongst the black Abyssinians. The Head Eunuch was the leader of all other black eunuchs and the Gynecium footmen. His rank was higher than the Esquire of the Sultan and would come after The Grand Vizier and Seyh-ül İslam (The head of Ottoman Muslims). The black Eunuchs would be classified as novices, Duty Assistant Master, Middle, and Master. One of those most experienced twelve masters would go up to the rank of The Transhumant Head Master first, to The new Imperial Gate Mastership later. The rank of Head Eunuch was their last stop.

It is understood that the number of white Eunuchs was larger than those of the blacks before. But, those white eunuchs were quite weak and would die a little after they were castrated. On the contrary, the black ones were strong and were able to do their job very well in the Harem. That's why they used to be preferred and had an irreplaceable status in

Darüssaade Master (Also named as the master of the girls) who was the master of the Hadım Ağalar (The masters of castration). From the album of Fenerci Mehmed "The Ottoman Clothes".

the Palace.

As the slave commerce brought in good money, some merchants used to kidnap black boys from Africa and had them castrated in castration centres. Those kidnapped children having been laid on a table first, tied up on the chest, the arms and the legs tightly. Then, their penises would be squeezed with a string and cut off using a sharp blade. They were screaming all during that brutal operation. Since the boy would die if there occurred some bleeding, the monks therefore would bind the cords and the veins to stop that. They would either put on some melted resin on the cut or cauterised it by a hot iron rod. Once it was done, some reeds would be inserted in their urethras to help urinating. Then, they were buried in the sand half way through their bodies. A few days later, they would be taken back in the Monastery by the monks and some aromatic oils would be applied on their cuts to continue healing. They could heal within a few months. But, all during that period those boys would feel an unbearable pain while urinating. The notorious place where the castration business was undertaken, was the Detr-el Abiad Monastery. The Arabs would have those black boys castrated by the monks of that Monastery and sell them to the merchants for very high prices. Most of those castrated boys would die. There were three castration methods;

The first one was; cutting off the balls and the penis, the second; cutting off the penis only, and the third one; cutting out the testicles. It was recorded that chopped off penises might grow again in some cases. With that probability, all the Eunuchs used to be checked by the Head Doctor periodically. If their penises were found growing they would immediately be kept away from the harem.

As the number of the black eunuchs increased in the harem, they formed a 'Eunuchs Guild' The black boys taken in that guild were raised by the elderly Eunuchs. The Imperial traditions would be taught both in theory and in practise. The training programme would be applied in a big discipline. Young black boys used to play with the other children in the Harem. The young black boys having arrived in the Harem, would be given some different names. The names they usually acquired were the names of flowers. Those learned black men used to be of service to the Sultana Mother, Princes, the wives of the Sultan too. Besides, they used to be sent to the homes of the Sultans' daughters which were outside the Palace. The Eunuchs used to stand on duty at the gate of the Harem and keep the entrance under their control. Also, they would either escort the doctor into the Harem or the residents leaving the Harem on carriages. The Eunuchs totally took over the management of the Harem after 1582. So, from that date on, Baltacılar (The Sappers) were given under their command. They could talk to the Sultan anytime they wanted to and organise the correspondence between the Sultan and the Grand Vizier. Because of their power and place in the Palace, some Eunuchs, as they had a word in the selection of the Grand Vizier, would intervene them in many ways.

A Eunuch of the Harem.
J.M. Véran.

A Eunuch of the Harem.
R. Simith.

On top of that, they were responsible for the foundations in Mecca and Medina called Haremeyn-i Şerifeyn. Their managing those foundations through regional directors made them become much more powerful in the Palace. Çadır Mehterbaşı (the Head of the Ottoman Army band), Hazinedar Usta (The Treasurer), Bezirgan Başı (The Trader), Peşkeşçibaşı (The official responsible for the presents given to the Sultan) were all given under his command. After all, their influence doubled in the Palace and they found themselves an important rank which was right after the The Grand Vizier and Şeyh-ül İslam (the Head of the Ottoman Muslims)in the protocol line.

The Eunuchs had their own wards by the carriage-gate of the Palace. The Head Eunuch had his chamber in that building, too. Harem Ağası also called 'Darüssade Ağası' (The Head Eunuch) used to manage the foundations in Saudi Arabia, obtain Concubines (women slaves) for the Harem and, inform the Sultan on İkbals' (The felicities), Kadın efendis' (Sultan's wives), Ustas' (Masters), Kalfas' (Assistant Masters) behaviours and activities and would get the Sultan to promote or punish them. Their duties would vary from the representation of the Sultanas in the wedding ceremonies to managing the wedding and his subjects in the Harem. Also, organising the Sürre Alayı(The Gift Procession sent to Medina and Mecca every year) was one of their posts.

When a Head Eunuch was dismissed, he would leave for Egypt for good. They were given a pension called 'Azatlık' to live on. Generally the new Sultan would appoint another Head Eunuch. Sometimes, they could keep their post despite the Sultan's replacement. We know that although some of those Head Eunuchs were illiterate, uneasy and over-sensitive they would still intervene the Imperial affairs as they were always backed up by the Sultan and his wives. The Head Eunuch, Hacı Mustafa Ağa served three Sultans in the Palace. He played a significant role in Mustafa I.'s dethronement. The Grand Vizier, İstanköylü Ali Pasha was fed up with him and exiled to Egypt. But, a while later he returned back to his previous post in the Palace. Soon after he had restarted his work he continued his interventions and sent out a fleet of the Ottoman navy to Crimea to replace the Crimean Khan Mehmet Giray with the previous Khan. The Kazakhs who were very angry with that came as far as the Bosphorus and destroyed Yeniköy. As a result, Mehmet Giray was able to keep his office and Hacı Mustafa Ağa died of his sorrow in 1624.

The Head Eunuch, Celali İbrahim Ağa who had played an active role in the assassination of the Sultan İbrahim was condemned to death for committing that crime in 1651. Turhan Valide Sultana's Head Lala (Manservant) Süleyman Ağa was promoted to the rank of the Head Eunuch since he had played an active role in the Kösem Sultana case. Having been proud of his new rank and strength, he started to intervene all the Imperial affairs. He had the Sultan appoint his friends to some high offices.

As he was not satisfied with what he had already done, he got the Sultan to dismiss the Grand Vizier Siyavuş Pasha. His passion was never ending. When he started having rows with Valide Turhan Sultana he was sent off to Egypt for good. We face with many of those

The Guard of the Harem, Jean-Léon Gérôme. The Wallace Collection, London.

either exiled to Egypt or killed because of their excessive interventions.

All those examples did not stop them and they always wanted to reach a higher office in the Empire. Uzun Süleyman Ağa was the Head

Eunuch during Ahmed III.'s sultanate, around the beginning of 18th. century. The Grand Vizier, Damat Hasan Pasha wanted to replace him with his own contact Treasurer Mehmet Ağa. Having learnt that, Süleyman Ağa influenced the Sultana Mother and the Sultan himself and had them dismiss the Grand Vizier instead. He had them replace him with his close friend Kalaylı Ahmed Pasha. Beşir Ağa is one of the most famous Eunuchs the Ottoman history recorded. The Grand Vizier İbrahim Pasha was fed up with his treatments in the Palace and asked the Sultan to dismiss him. The Sultan Mahmud I. decided to dismiss him at first. But, Beşir Ağa went to plead the Sultana Mother who later had a word with the Sultan about his dismissal and asked him to keep Beşir Ağa in the Palace. The Sultan did not agree with his mother in the beginning but as she said to his son 'I am never going to forgive you for that' he had to accept her request. And, upon her request he had to dismiss the Grand Vizier İbrahim Pasha. After Hacı Beşir Ağa, there came Beşir Ağa as the Head Eunuch. He was the follower of the previous Eunuch Hacı Beşir Ağa and always wanted to act out as he had done before. But, the Sultan of the time had his head chopped off, and thus their influence came to an end in the Palace. Beside those mean Eunuchs, there lived some trustworthy, good-hearted ones, too.

The Sultana Mothers

The mothers of the Sultans were called Sultana Mothers. This term was first used for the mother of the Sultan Murad III and then it became a tradition to call them 'The Sultana Mother'. When Murad III moved the old palace from Bayezıd to The Topkapı Palace his mother came in with him and settled in the Harem, becoming the number one woman of the Harem. Since the time of Murad III the Sultana Mother's relocation in the new Palace was escorted by Valide Alayı (The Sultana Mother procession). After his girding on the sword, the new Sultan would order his mother to be escorted to the new Palace. A few days later, the procession would start from the old palace. She would either get on 'the flying throne' or a horse-drawn carriage. The Ottoman soldiers would line up on both sides of the road to greet the Sultana Mother.

When the Sultana Mother procession arrived outside the baker's in the first courtyard, the Sultan would open the door of the carriage and take her out by kissing her hand and escort her to the Harem. The Sultan's Concubines would also be escorted to the Harem from the old Palace, and sometimes there would a convoy of one hundred carriages. On the second day upon her arrival at the Harem, the Grand Vizier would be informed of the event. The Grand Vizier would be honoured with a fur coat and a precious dagger. The Grand Vizier would welcome the new comers at the Pasha gate and read out the decree of the Sultan. Then, by wearing that fur coat, he would give out his presents to the ones who had brought them in return. The chamber the Sultana Mother used to live in, was the second largest one after the Sultan's. There used to be a vast sultana courtyard and their chamber

The Sultana Mother, Nurbanu Sultana , the mother of Murad III was buried at the sepulchre of Selim II at St. Sophia.

would open into that. The downstairs was for their Concubines (Women slaves) serving them. Those places would be heated by braziers filled up with glowing fire brought from The Sultana Mother's fireplace. Their fireplaces were decorated with unique china. There used to be three floors. They would usually live on the ground floor, eat and perform their prayers on the first floor and sleep on the top floor. The Sultana Mother chamber had a waiting room right outside the entrance. Guards would stand on duty at the entrance. The stairs opposite the guards would lead up to the rooms of the Sultana Mother. At the Sultana Mother's Hamam (Turkish Bath), the Sultana Mother herself, her maids, the Sultan's wives and his favourites would bathe. Also, the Concubine (Female slave) offered to the Sultan by the Sultana Mother or the Head Eunuch would bathe and set off elegantly there, too. By the hidden passage she would be escorted to the Sultan's chamber from the Hamam. On her way back she would be taken into one of the rooms on the top floor of the Sultana Mother's chamber. Once she was settled in there, she would be checked if she had got pregnant. If so, she would permanently hold her own chamber as a Kadın Efendi(The Wife of the Sultan). The Sultana Mother chamber was built in the 16th. century. Its walls were all covered with china and there used to be a large hall with a nice fireplace used as the living room. That vast Valide hall lost its originality after being restored many times. The icons on its dome were the art of the 18th. century. After that vast hall there came three rooms, the first one of which was covered with enamelled tiles, was the Sultana Mother's bedroom. The next room covered with Mecca style china was used as the prayers room. Another room was added by the windows of that room later on.

After his accession to the throne, Selim III had

the architect Melling build two separate rooms on the mezzanine floor; one for his mother and the other for his love affairs.

Nurbanu Sultana, Safiye Sultana, Kösem Sultana, Turhan Sultana and Nakşidil Sultana were the ones whose names have always been remembered. The Sultana Mother, Nurbanu, the mother of Murad III and the wife of Selim II was the first Sultana Mother who lived and died in that new Palace.

The mother of Ahmed I, The Sultana Mother, Handan; the mother of Süleyman II, The Sultana Mother, Dilasub; the mother of Ahmed III and Mustafa II, The Sultana Mother, Gülnuş; the mother of Mahmud I, The Sultana Mother, Saliha; the mother of Osman III, The Sultana Mother, Şehsuvar; the mother of Mahmud II, The Sultana Mother, Nakşidil were the ones who lived in that chamber when

their sons were the Sultans of the Ottomans. The last settler of the chamber was The Sultan Abdülmecid's mother, The Sultana Mother, Pertevniyal Valide Sultan. After her, all The Sultana Mothers lived in the Dolmabahçe Palace.

The Sultana Mothers , as they had very fertile lands were able to make good money. They used to have their Kethüdas (Assistants) manage their property. With their income they would have many fountains and mosques built. At the same time, they founded charities, too. They used to have many Concubines (Women slaves) around them. The Sultana Mother would manage all the affairs in the Harem with the help of Hazinedar Usta (The Treasurer). All other residents of the Harem such as, the Wives of the Sultan, Masters, Concubines had to respect the Treasurer.

Coffee serving in the Harem had a rule. Whenever a Sultana Mother wanted his son to see a concubine, she would, then, send out her to serve coffee to the Sultan. A painting illustrating the event exists in the Demirbank collection.

Coffee serving to the Sultan's wife and his favourites in the courtyard, a painting by Amedee Van Loo.

ROSSA SOLYMANNI
VXOR..

Hürrem Sultana

Upon his father Yavuz Sultan Selim's death in 1520, Süleyman sat on the Ottoman throne which would last for 46 years. His legacy to his country and people was great. That's why he has always been named as Sultan Süleyman, the magnificent. His saying, still well-known in Turkey, is a proof of his legacy "There is not such a thing as honourable as the State for my public, but no state on Earth is more important than one of them". He was very well educated, tactful and ruled his country attentively. He had continuous victories from one front to the other. He had the world accept his greatness with his strength and legacy. This Sultan, at the age 26, while walking up the steps of his historical improvement, met that Concubine who would change his destiny afterwards.

Upon his arrival from the Belgrade Battle he wanted to pass a good night at the Harem with a beautiful slave. All the Concubines were informed of his decision and started to prepare themselves for that great Emperor. To be selected by the Sultan, all of them wanted to be the most beautiful one. The one who was selected might be the most honourable woman of the Palace. They were informed of his arrival. All of them immediately stood in a row and started to wait for the Sultan to walk past them.

Finally, the Sultan turned up. As all of them kept their eyes on the ground, that red-haired, sharp-nosed, white-tanned beauty with a voluptuous body gazed at the Sultan. He could

Hürrem Sultana who stole Sultan Süleyman's heart had started off from scratch as an ordinary concubine.

The painting of Sultan Süleyman magnificent.

not take his eyes off that beauty. He bowed and whispered into the Treasurer Master's ear "I want to spend the night with her". He asked him to send her to his room at night. That slave woman was originally from Russia, the daughter of the monk of Rutenya. Her name was Alexandra. At the time of Yavuz Sultan Selim, she was captured as a Prisoner of War by the Crimean Turks and sold to the Grand Vizier Makbul İbrahim Pasha. He had the officials educate her and gave her to the Sultana Mother Hafsa Sultana who later delivered her at the Harem. She was named Hürrem Sultana but widely known by the western world as Roxselane.

In that evening , she was bathed, put on good scents and sent to the Sultan. She was only seventeen when she first met the Sultan in his bed. She had to do her best to have the Sultan like her. It was the most important night in her life, actually it was exactly a "to be or not to be" night for her; The Sultan would either like her or send her back to continue the rest of her life as an ordinary woman slave in the Harem. She had to be liked there was no other way out. So, she tried to do her best that night. At dawn, the presents the Sultan had left in the room was the sign of his appreciation. She was successful and was able to attract the Sultan's attention. And, as the Sultan wanted to see her once again, she found herself as the most favourite woman of the Harem overnight. A little later, she got pregnant and gave birth. After the birth she deliberately wanted to leave the Palace knowing that she was going to be stopped. As she had thought, the Sultan Süleyman did not want her to leave the Palace. She was convinced to stay in after he officially married her which was

contrary to the Imperial traditions of the time. His love for Hürrem made his first wife Mahidevran very angry. A dispute which would last for quite a long time started between the two ladies in the Palace. At times, although Hafsa Sultana wanted to stop that dispute, they had already reached the road of no return.

Finally, the two women fought in the Harem and went up to the Sultan for complaints. The both, exaggerating their bites and cuts wanted to play the innocent. Who do you think was successful? It was Hürrem , of course, who was successful in the role play. Their dispute came to end as Süleyman sent Mahidevran Sultana off to Manisa. The Sultana Mother, Hafsa Sultana died, leaving Hürrem the chance to become the starlet in the Palace. She did not have the intention of missing that chance and became the sole possessor of the Harem. One after another, she gave birth to baby-sons named; Mehmet, Selim, Beyazid and Cihangir. That foxy, playful belle made the Sultan fall in love with her. Whenever Sultan Süleyman was away for a war she used to write long letters expressing her great love to him. She always started her letters, stating "My Sultan, piece of my heart, the sun of my state, the star of my happiness, his Majesty". Her letters would effect the Sultan deep in his heart. Of course, Sultan Süleyman was replying her letters eagerly which were full of love and her appreciation. He would ·start his letters to Hürrem by saying "The throne of my lonely corner, my sweetheart, my sincere, intimate friend, my moonlight, the queen of beauties".

Sultan Süleyman brought a slave named İbrahim as he liked the way he had played the violin . He was a Prince in Manisa , then. They were at the same age. Sultan Süleyman was impressed by that slave in many ways. As he was coming to Istanbul, he asked İbrahim to accompany him. He gave him the title 'Pasha' and later appointed him as the Grand Vizier. He was known as Makbul İbrahim Pasha. Sultan Süleyman, the Magnificent married her sister, Hatice Sultana to İbrahim and gave them a mansion he recently had it built in Sultanahmet.

Hürrem was ruthless. While she was taking the steps with a great confidence, discarding anyone who might create problems for her. She was completely done except İbrahim Pasha. He was the only man in the Palace she could not persuade. She became jealous of her husband's affection to that guy, too. İbrahim Pasha was also supporting Mahidevran's son Mustafa. That's why she had to discard the man hindering her plans.

Her husband Sultan Süleyman was always defending him on anything he did. So, she had to wait until he took a false step. She did so and waited. She was incredibly patient, too. To keep the balance against İbrahim Pasha, his wife Hatice Sultana and Prince Mustafa, she had to marry her daughter to someone so strong so that she could form a real pact. The Governor General to Diyarbakır, Rüstem Pasha was an exceptional opportunity. They had a perfect trio after the marriage. Her target was to have her chemical sons sit on the throne after The Magnificent. But, Prince Mustafa had to be discarded. Actually, before him, she had to have İbrahim Pasha killed. To her, İbrahim Pasha was too much spoilt by the Sultan. Although he was married to the Sultan's daughter, he had a secret mistress and would write letters to her. On one of his trips to Iraq he wrote two letters; one for the wife and the other for the lover. Unfortunately, somehow, those letters reached at the wrong addresses. The wife having

Mihrimah Sultana, the daughter of Sultan Süleyman the Magnificent from Hürrem Sultana. She was married to Rüstem Pasha and became her father's best friend after her mother's death. Rahmi Koç Collection, Istanbul.

received the letter written to the lover got incredibly angry and the Palace did not welcome the incident. Also, İbrahim Pasa's saying to an envoy "My word is more authoritative than that of the Sultan" prepared his end. As a climax, when he signed a document as 'The Minister of War' the Sultan was convinced by Hürrem that he had to be killed. Some letters were also said to be found on his secret agreement with the German Emperor Charl V. Hürrem was not late to strike the final blow. Sultan Süleyman was totally convinced that he was a traitor. He invited İbrahim Pasha for a dinner at the Palace one night. When he went to his room for the night he had already ordered the executioners to kill him. He was strangled by those executioners in his bed. Hürrem was more than happy upon her rival's death. There left nobody in the Palace to defend Prince Mustafa. So, it was his turn. She had to be patient and play everything by the ear. First of all, she had to find an appropriate candidate for the rank of the Grand Vizier. Rüstem Pasha was ideal for the post and he was the son-in-law of the Sultan, too. With the great help of Hürrem, he became the Grand Vizier. It was time for Mustafa to be in disgrace.

Imperial women would wear aigrettes on their heads.

She sent out Rüstem Pasha's men to work in close contact with him. That way she was able to get any information on his movements. She worked as a detective. By taking over the letters Mustafa had written to his father, sent them to the Sultan by changing the content. She did the same with the Sultan's letters to Mustafa too. She always picked the Sultan's letters up and sent them to his son after rewriting them the way she had liked to. The tension was at the peak. The letters from the Sultan saying "Do not stand against the State my boy!" never reached to its address. And the letters he had written to his father were all lost on the way to their address. The Sultan had wanted to go to talk to his son personally but was convinced by Hürrem that it would be inappropriate for a Sultan to go to talk to his son. So, he sent out Rüstem Pasha to have a word with him. That was Hürrem's plan, of course. She had known that Rüstem Pasha could be the one the Sultan would send to talk to Mustafa in his name. That's why she had to convince him on that. So, Rüstem Pasha went to see his son. They had a short meeting. Having returned back in the palace he went to brief about his appointment with Mustafa. Nobody could have expected him to say anything Mustafa had performed correctly. So, he told the Sultan that he had been planning to dethrone him by provoking the public. Whereas, he did not have such an intention. That was a lie and it had to be presented to the Sultan that way. Finally, Süleyman gave his decision; He would lose his son for sake of the State and the regulations of the Empire. But, how was he going to put up with the loss of his second son?

In the year 1553, Rüstem Pasha set off for a war in Iran. Sultan Süleyman followed him with the Governor of Manisa and his unhealthy son Cihangir. His other son Beyazid was in Karaman. He ordered Mustafa to join the army. Everyone had already been aware of his intentions. Mustafa was beloved by all the members of the Military and the public. He was warned about his father's intention. They pleaded him not to go since there would be a trap waiting for him. The second Grand Vizier Ahmed Pasha instructed him not to leave Amasya. He said "Even if I am going for my death, I will still go. He is the one who gave me my life and let him the one to take my life back, too. I am going to confront my father. He is my father, he is going to listen to me". He set off with his army of 5000 soldiers. Sultan Süleyman's headquarters was around Aktepe near Konya. Mustafa's army put up their tents about three kilometres away from where his father was. Everyone was coming into his tent to persuade him not to go to his father's tent. Even a piece of paper attached to an arrow shot on his tent bearing; "Do not go to your father's tent or else you will get killed." He said again "Even if this is true, he gave me my life and he is going to take it back" Right outside the tent, as per the tradition, he delivered his dagger to one of Süleyman's warriors and walked into. Seven dumb executioners were waiting for him inside. Soon after he had got in they put their ropes around his neck. He fought bravely but an executioner named Zal Mahmud, approaching him from behind strangled him. They put his corpse outside the tent. Cihangir, although he was the son of Hürrem adored Mustafa. He froze to death when he saw his brother's corpse lying outside the tent. Mustafa's murder created a pall mall in the army. All the soldiers did not eat or drink anything that day. They were all booing and shouting against the Sultan and Hürrem. Protests never stopped. They wanted the ones who had been involved in the murder to be punished. Mustafa's close friend poet Taşlıcalı Yahya wrote an elegy upon his murder starting with the lines ; "Some part of the Earth has been terminated, the predestinated moment of death took our prince away" That elegy was at everybody's tongue and they all wanted the Sultan to dismiss Rüstem Pasha. Sultan Süleyman could not resist his army and the public anymore and had to replace him with the second Vizier Ahmed Pasha, the husband of his sister Fatma Sultana. When the army arrived in Aleppo, Cihangir had already died of his sorrow. His death shook Sultan Süleyman deeply. Cihangir, died at the age of 22, was buried at Mehmed's tomb by the Şehzade Mosque. He had the Cihangir Mosque built to his memory but could not cease his sorrow.

He secluded himself totally. Having devoted himself to religion at the same time, he had Mimar Sinan build Süleymaniye. Hürrem also

An aigrette Hürrem Sultana wore.

calmed down and she devoted herself to religion, too. Because she had nobody to stop her anymore. She had Mimar Sinan build the twin Hamams across St.Sophia and the Haseki Institution at Avrat Pazarı. Her son-in-law Rüstem Pasha had already lost his popularity.

The ceremonial caftan of Sultan Süleyman the Magnificent.

She was able to save his life by pleading Sultan Süleyman. She could not impose anything on the new Grand Vizier, Ahmet Pasha. There passed two years, it was 1554 when the people congregated around a man who was alike Prince Mustafa in many ways and revolted against the Sultan. In fact, Prince Beyazid had been behind that revolt which was ended by Sultan Süleyman.

After the revolt, Hürrem got another chance to return to her old days. She convinced Sultan Süleyman that Ahmed Pasha had been behind that revolt. Ahmed Pasha had always held Hürrem and Rüstem Pasha responsible for the death of Mustafa. When Mustafa was killed he had to accept the rank of the Grand Vizier by force. Sultan Süleyman appointed Kara Ahmed Pasha, compromising in many things, as the Grand Vizier. He swore that he would not take his seal back until he died. The nervousness in the army halted after his becoming the Grand Vizier. Hürrem wanted Sultan Süleyman to dismiss him but as he had sworn he could not have stepped back. But, that was Hürrem, of course. She finally found a way to get rid of him. She went to Sutan Süleyman and said "You swore not to take his seal back until he died, so neither dismiss him nor take his seal back, just kill him". Sultan Süleyman was convinced. So, he ordered his executioners to kill him. After he had been killed Rüstem Pasha became the Grand Vizier once again.

The caftan of the son of Sultan Süleyman the Magnificent, Prince Mehmed who died at a very early age. His death upset Sultan Süleyman the Magnificent so much that he had the Prince Mehmed Mosque built to his memory.

Hürrem finally got rid of all her rivals. But, this time her two sons could not get on well. There was an incredible dispute in between the two boys. Beyazid was after his father, that's why Hürrem loved him very much. He was a good poet, brave and had a good character. He was also deeply loved by the army too. Nobody liked Selim, though. The throne would either belong to Selim or Beyazid. Now, she was at the crossroads, she had only two roads. All she had was her two boys in her life. Since she had

everyone around her killed, she did not have anybody else except them. Who did she have to support this time? Against Mustafa, she had always supported her son Selim, but that time it was different. Before she saw the fight between her two boys she had got ill in Edirne and brought to Istanbul. It was impossible for her to get well because of the illness she had. And, she died in April 1558 at the age of 54. She was buried at her tomb by the Süleymaniye Mosque. After her death the dispute between Beyazid and Selim increasingly continued. Beyazid, with his army, marched on to fight Selim. Sultan Süleyman took the incident as a revolt against the State and declared him as a rebel. Beyazid got defeated and was strangled in Iran by the Sultan's executioners. Having left thousands of dead bodies behind, Sultan Süleyman was able to keep the Empire united. Unfortunately, two of those dead bodies were his own sons. Rüstem Pasha having served for 15 years died, too. There remained her daughter, Mihrimah Sultana only who would be with him all the time.

On one of those days he felt so lonely, he was waiting for one of his wives named Gülfem in the Harem. But, as she had desperately needed money for the mosque she had been donating for its construction, she had to sell her turn to some other woman. Instead of Gülfem, when he saw some other woman turn up, he got very angry and ordered her to be killed. He said it was against the Sultanate. But, he later found

out that, she had done it to be able to finish the construction of that mosque. He got very miserable indeed and ordered his subordinates to finish the construction of the mosque. He had been governing his country for 46 years. Although he was 72 he had already been worn out, collapsed and lost all his enthusiasm. He hadn't been away for a war for ten years. The Grand Vizier, Sokollu Mehmed Pasha was insisting on his setting off for a war. So, with his participation, the Ottoman army set off for a war at the beginning of May in the year 1566. The army arrived in Zigetvar around the beginning of August. They surrounded the castle, fought for days but it did not fall. His health was deteriorating day by day.

And, Sultan Süleyman, the Magnificent died on September 6th. 1566. His commanders hid the news of his death from the army for the success of the siege. But, Prince Selim had already been informed to sit on the throne in Istanbul. After he had sat on the throne his death was announced to the public. They built a tomb for him in Zigetvar and buried his internal organs. But, his real sepulchre was built by the Süleymaniye Mosque in Istanbul. He had spent ten years three months and five days of his 46-year-long sultanate on battlefields and demolished his two sons for the State, the regulations and the laws of the Empire. And, the era of that 46-year-long sultanate was over.

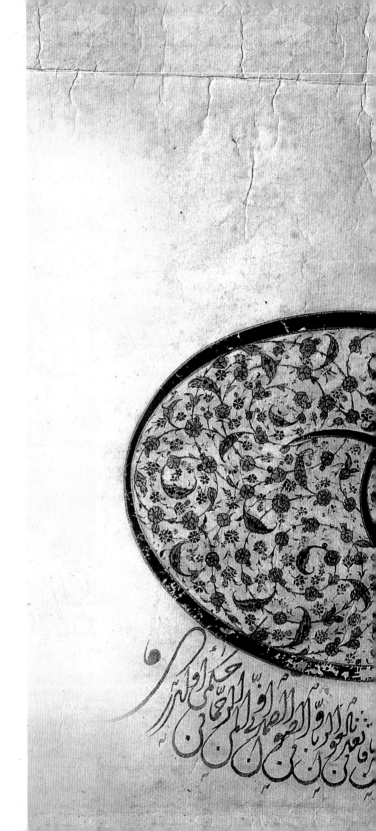

The Tuğra (seal) of Sultan Süleyman the Magnificent,
The Museum at the Topkapı Palace.

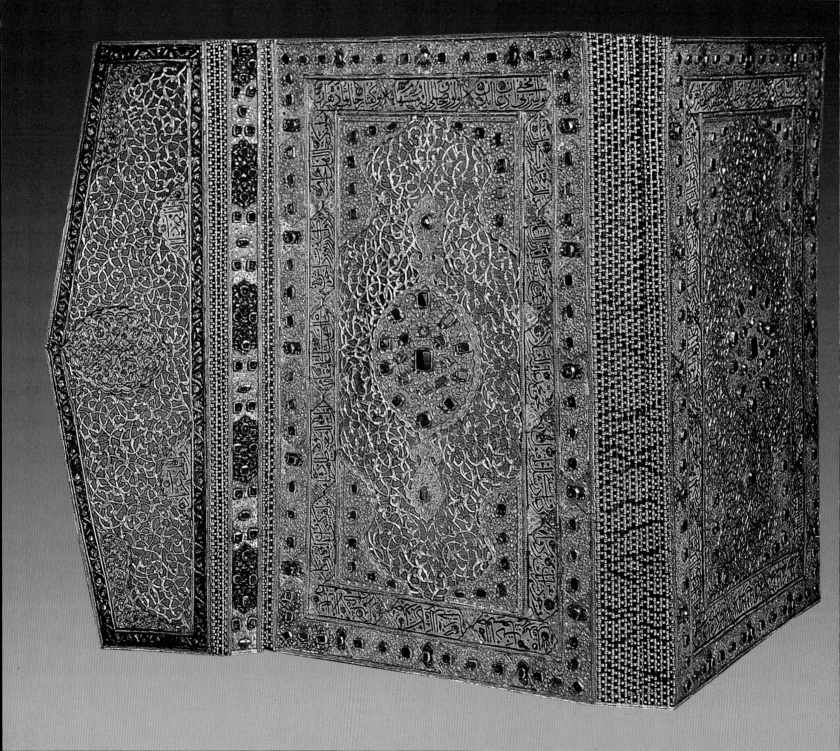

Safiye Sultana

Safiye Sultana was from the Baffo family of Venice. Her father was the governor to the Corfu Island of the Republic of Venice. The ship she was on was captured by some Turkish pirates in the Adriatic on her way to Venice. That 14-year-old girl was given to Prince Murad as a gift who was in Manisa at that time. He really liked the girl very much and after sitting on the Ottoman throne in 1574 with the title Murad III, he took her to the Palace in Istanbul as his first wife. Her name had already been changed to Safiye and she had been taught the Islamic rules before going to the Palace. But, the Sultana Mother, Nurbanu and Safiye started to have some dispute. The sisters of the Sultan were of course on their mother's side.

To disgrace her, they would offer the Sultan young and beautiful Concubines. They also encouraged him to have children from other Concubines since Safiye Sultana's children had all died. Murad III started to have some affairs with the Concubines offered himself one after another. Sultan Murad had some intercourse with one Concubine offered him by his sister İsmihan Sultana for the first time, then the others followed. Safiye Sultana had resisted that at first, but since that was an inevitable result, she had to put up with it and keep her mouth shut. Murad III had been the only one of all the Sultans who was extremely fond of women. As he had started to have some other affairs with Concubines almost everyday, he nearly forgot Safiye Sultana. He is even said to have been with some other women outside the Palace, too. He was a real vagabond.

The golden case consisting of the poems of Murad III, the husband of Safiye Sultana.

The portrait of Murad III.

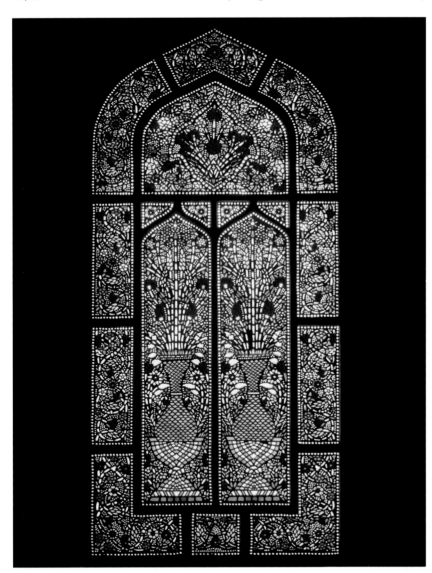

Windows in coloured glass in the chamber of the wives of the Sultans. Those windows in the Harem reflect the women's taste.

But, Safiye Sultana became the top woman of the Palace upon Nurbanu's death in 1585. She was not jealous of his husband anymore and even let him do anything he wanted to. She totally devoted herself to the internal and the external affairs of the Ottoman Empire which she enjoyed doing very much. Since her son Mehmed III ascended to the throne upon his father's death in 1595, she doubled her influence with her new rank of 'the Sultana Mother'. She would treat her daughter-in-law, Handan Sultana as if she was one of her Concubines. She was the absolute authority of the Empire. She would appoint anybody she liked to, to any post. Whoever greased her palm the most, would get a better position. The rules, the ethics of the Empire, Sultan Süleyman had set, were completely shattering. Her bribery affairs were managed by the Gate Footman Gazanfer Ağa, the Girls' Footman Osman Ağa, Raziye Hatun and the Jewish expatriate, Ester Kira. Through Ester Kira she would contact the Venetian Ambassador and collect bribes from the customs. In 1600, Safiye had Kira coin some debased money planning to give them to the Ottoman soldiers. The soldiers soon realised that the coins they received were abnormal. So, all the soldiers rebelled. To them, the one who was responsible for that was Kira herself. As Safiye had always been behind the curtain, she was able to sneak out of the incident. So, they killed Kira and her son. She already started to lose her partners. She had been playing so carefully and cleverly that she did not become their target. A few years later, the soldiers rebelled again and killed the Gate Footman Gazanfer Ağa and the Girls' Footman Osman Ağa as they had been found guilty by them. She lost two more partners in that rebellion. She had been twisting her son Mehmed III around her little finger. But, the people in Anatolia were under a brutal reign of the Governors who had taken those offices by the power of their money. Thus, nobody could put up with the situation anymore in Anatolia. They said they had nothing to give out but their lives only. The Anatolian people rebelled all over Anatolia against their governors. That incident was called The Celali Rebellion. Mehmed III. sent out armies one after another to stop the rebellion but, all their troops were defeated against the power of the public. His 21-year-old son, Mahmud asked him if he could lead his own army to overwhelm the rebellion in Anatolia. He said 'Dad, appoint me as the commander in chief so that I will overcome this rebellion in Anatolia' But, Safiye convinced her husband that his son had his eye on his throne. She said to him that he was chasing after victories which could open him the gates to his Sultanate. Nobody could expect him to take another step his mother did not approve of. So, one night while he was asleep, the Sultan's executioners strangled him to death. Safiye Sultana started the construction of the Yeni Cami (Yeni Mosque) in Eminönü but the public did not welcome the idea since they knew the monies being spent for that construction, had come from bribery.

That weak sovereignty which had lasted for 13 years ended upon Mehmed III.'s death at the age of 37 in 1603. His grandson Ahmed sat on the throne after him and sent Safiye Sultana to the old Palace. After having been exiled in the old palace for two years, Safiye Sultana died in 1605 and was buried at her husband's sepulchre at St. Sophia.

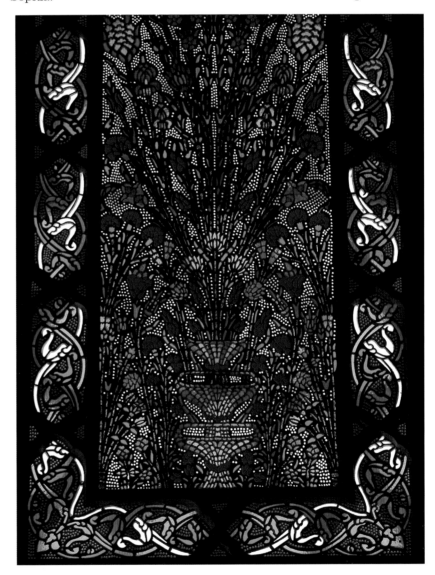

The windows at the chamber of the Ottoman Princes were also adorned with coloured glass.

Kösem and Turhan Sultanas

Ahmed I was still a child when he became the Sultan at the beginning of the 17th. century. He sent Safiye Sultana to the old Palace and appointed his mother Handan Sultana to the rank of The Sultana Mother. Handan Sultana suffered a lot. Unfortunately, she died two years later since she had had a very tough time created by Safiye Sultana. That young Sultan had a favourite wife called Mahfiruz Sultana. She had a very quiet and a happy life until 1609 and gave birth to 4 babies named, Mehmed, Süleyman, Beyazid and Hüseyin. But, on Mahpeyker Sultana's (known as Kösem Sultana) going into the Sultan's life, everything changed. Kösem Sultana gave birth to a baby son named Murad IV. So, another dispute started in the Harem. She had been presented to the Palace at the age of 12 or 13 by the Bosnian Pasha and she was given a Turkish name, Mahpeyker. She attracted everybody's attention, especially the Sultan's, with her beauty and intelligence. After Murad, her giving birth to Süleyman, İbrahim, Kasım, Ayşe and Fatma made her the most authorised woman of the Harem.

Ahmed I, as a teenager, ruled his country for 14 years and died at the age of 27. He was buried in a sepulchre by the Sultanahmet Mosque. As a tradition when the Sultan died his eldest son would sit on the throne. In that case, Mahfiruz Sultana's son Osman would ascend to the throne and, she herself would become the Sultana Mother. Then, of course, Kösem Sultana would be sent out of the Harem by the Sultana Mother.

The Sultanahmet Mosque and its tomb.

When Kösem Sultana died, she was buried at the tomb by the mosque her husband Ahmed I had it built to her memory.

Kösem Sultana immediately started to send some presents to the ones who had the authority in the Palace to be able to have the Sultan's brother Mustafa ascend to the throne. She worked so hard to achieve her goal. As Mustafa was insane, Ahmed I had not touched him and let him live in the Harem his way. So, the high rank officials in the Palace after having been bribed by Kösem, made Mustafa sit on the throne despite the traditions. Kösem thought of managing him in all ways. And, she thought that, in the meantime her boys would grow up to take over the throne. She could have her executioners kill Mahfiruz's son Osman within time as well. The only thing she had not considered was the sudden deterioration of Mustafa's health. The Girls' Footman Hacı Mustafa Ağa was no longer able to put up with his craziness. He locked him up in his room and had Mustafa sit on the throne. So, Genç Osman to be known as Osman II. later, became the Sultan.

He was at the age of 14 only. Mahfiruz became the Sultana Mother and Kösem was exiled in the old Palace. It had not taken long for Mahfiruz to reign as the Sultana Mother as she died 3 years after his son's accession to the throne. Kösem had been trying hard in the old Palace to dethrone Genç Osman. She threatened the officials in Palace as well as the army commanders saying that their heads would be cut off if they couldn't dethrone Genç Osman. So, the army rebelled against the Sultan. Genç Osman was dethroned and strangled to death at the Yedikule prison. So, Sultan Mustafa regained his throne. Kösem's plans were successful as she had exterminated Genç Osman. What she had to do was to wait until her eldest son grow up to become the Sultan. But, as Mustafa's craziness was unbearable, she could not wait any longer and made her 12-year-old son Murad IV sit on the throne. She returned back in the Palace with a glorious parade. She was quite comfortable as the Sultana Mother. Since Murad IV. did not have any experience on governmental issues, Kösem Sultana governed the State for the following ten years. Murad IV., until he reached the age of 22, did not open his mouth to say anything to whatever his mother had done. Especially when he was away for a war, Kösem would totally take over all the State affairs. Murad IV, upon returning back from the Baghdad battle very sick, died very young leaving the throne to his brother İbrahim. Her reign continued as Ibrahim, her other son, took over the throne after the death of Murad IV. İbrahim was paranoid since he had always been scared of being killed. Kösem did not have any other sons to send to the throne after him. So, She started to present him with beautiful Concubines every single day.

Hatice Turhan was born in Russia. She was enslaved by the Tartars and given to Kösem as a gift by the Blind Süleyman Pasha. Kösem Sultana trained her very fast and gave her to İbrahim who was fascinated by her beauty. She was white-tanned, tall, thin and a real belle. Turhan Sultana gàve birth to a baby son named Mehmed. It did not take Turhan Sultana long to become the Sultana Mother since his son Mehmet IV. had ascended to the throne at the age of seven upon İbrahim's dethronement. She was only 21 and very inexperienced and so, Kösem Sultana continued her efficiency on all matters. A while later, both of them started an authorisation struggle in the Palace. Kösem Sultana had already lost her control over Turhan Sultana. So, she started planning to help Süleyman whose

Murad IV, the son of Kösem Sultana was able to set the authority after sitting on the throne at an early age.

mother was a bit insane, become the Sultan in place of Mehmed IV. As some Cariye had informed Turhan Sultana on her plans, she was strangled to death by the Eunuchs. Kösem's reign which had lasted for 30 years came to an end. So, it was Turhan Sultana's turn. That time, she was the absolute ruler of the State as her son was quite young. She was always under the influence of the Girls' Footman Uzun Süleyman Ağa and Meleki Kalfa as they had contributed in Kösem's death. Although she had good intentions on anything, she had to govern the State as per their requests. Bribery and embezzlement grew in the Palace. Since everything based upon bribery, inexperienced people had already taken over the important offices throughout the Empire by sake of their money.

Turhan Sultana was very honest and kindhearted. She soon realised what her counterparts had been doing. With the recommendation of Kasım Ağa, she immediately appointed Köprülü Mehmed Pasha to the rank of the Grand Vizier. She wanted him to regain the honour, dignity and the ethics the Empire had lost. By sake of him, State affairs were all set on honesty and equality. So, the women's interference in the state affairs ended with Turhan Sultana's clever decision of appointing Köprülü to the rank of the Grand Vizier. Turhan Sultana started to sit in a corner and devote herself to religion.

In 1660, with her own income, she had the castles in Çanakkale (The Dardanelles) built and the Yeni Mosque in Istanbul completed, the contruction of which had been started by Safiye Sultana before. When she died in 1683, was buried in the sepulchre by the Yeni Mosque.

One of Turhan Sultana's foundations. A painting by Jean Baptiste Hilair at the Louvre Museum illustrating the sultan and his wives having dinner.

Gülnuş Sultana

Mehmed IV's head wife Gülnuş Sultana was born in Crete in 1642. She was a member of the Verzini family. The Commander-in-Chief Deli Hüseyin Pasha enslaved that beautiful girl after he had conquered the city of Resmo. He gave her to the Harem as a gift. According to the Imperial traditions her name was changed to Gülnuş. She had a tanned skin, dark hair. Upon concluding the training period she was introduced to the Sultan. He really liked that plump, brunette belle. Her flirtatious approach made Mehmed IV fall in love with her so soon. She empowered her status after giving birth to Prince Mustafa and Prince Ahmed. Gülnuş Sultana was in love with the Sultan too. Within time, the Sultan started to like another Cariye named Gülbeyaz. She was more than furious after she had learnt about it. One day, she organised a picnic by the sea and invited all the Concubines. While Gülbeyaz was sitting on a rock she pushed her off the cliff. She got on well with her mother-in-law, Turhan Sultana and upon her death she became the absolute ruler of the Harem. She never went into political affairs. Her hobby was hunting. She would go for long hunting parties organised by the husband. She was fond of Edirne where she used to pass most of her time as much as she could.

During his 39-year-long reign, which started when he was at the age of 7, Mehmed IV had some other women beside Gülbeyaz. Afife, the best poet after Hürrem, was his latest woman. As Mehmed IV was also interested in poetry, and had quite a refined personality, they loved each other. Her love in literature made him fall in love with her deeply. Their interest collided with one another's. By using

Gülnuş Sultana promoted to the rank of the Sultana Mother upon her sons, Ahmed and Mustafa's ascending to the throne respectively.

The portrait of Mehmed IV, the husband of Gülnuş Sultana.

the power of the words they started to impress each other. They would write one another letters full of poems telling about their love. In all his letters and poems, he would praise Afife's beauty and reveal his love deeply.

In one of his letters he addressed to Afife, he wrote;

"My sweet Afife you look like a rose"

During his long reign the Grand Vizier Köprülü Mehmet Pasha who had replaced Tarhuncu Pasha was able to set the authorisation of the Empire again. During his service, Mehmed IV was quite comfortable and laid back since the authority all over the Empire was set in. But, the Grand Viziers after Köprülü Mehmed Pasha were not efficient

The Sultans and their women would take boat trips on the Bosphorus. Those boats are illustrated in front of the Çırağan Palace and the Topkapı Palace.

enough. As a result, defeats, disappointments, turmoil started to appear all over the Empire. He was not interested in anything else but hunting only. The army held him responsible for all the defeats and wanted him to leave the throne. So, with his two sons 23 year-old Mustafa and 14 year-old Ahmed, he was exiled in the houses located in a remote part of the Topkapı Palace overlooking the Marmara Sea in November 1687. Süleyman II sat on the throne upon his dethronement. His lover Afife got very miserable with his exile and she even wrote a poem for the incident.

" Tell Gülnuş to dress up in black
    And die in sorrow with every breath.
    Sultan Mehmed crying in Şimşirlik
    Says 'Alas! A little sympathy on me"

Mehmed IV also known as Mehmet, the Hunter, wanted Afife and Gülnuş Sultanas to be sent in to live with him. But, Süleyman did not approve it and sent them to the old palace instead. Ahmed II ascended to the throne after Süleyman II. Following their short term sultanates, Mustafa II sat on the Ottoman throne. His mother Gülnuş Sultana returned back in the Harem as the Sultana Mother in the year 1695. Mustafa II died at a very young age and the Ottoman throne was kept by Ahmed III, the youngest son of Gülnuş Sultana this time. In the mean time, her authority as the Sultana Mother continued. So, the Harem passed 60 years under her authority as a Sultana Mother. She was one of the long-lasted Sultana Mothers in the Ottoman history. She died in Edirne in 1715. Her corpse was brought to Istanbul and buried at the sepulchre in front of the Üsküdar Mosque.

The Sultans would use some precious hangings. The picture of one of those hangings ornamented with emeralds.

Abdülhamid I and Ruhşah

Upon Mustafa III's death, his brother Abdülhamid ascended to the throne on Friday, January 21st. 1774 at the age of 49. That new Sultan was religious, kindhearted and tolerant and his public loved him as he had those qualities.

We know that he had several wives named, Ayşe Sineperver, Binnaz, Dilpezir, Humaşah, Mehtabe, Mislinayah, Nakşidil, Nevres, Şebisefa and Ruhşah Sultanas. Abdülhamid used to stay in a room opposite the Hünkar Hamamı (The Sultan's Bath) in the Harem decorated with Turkish style architecture. Osman II had had that room built and Abdülhamid used it after having it restored. Besides, he had a two storey Gözdeler (The Favourites) chamber built to separate his wives from the Favourites. It was at the remote end of the Harem in Topkapı Palace

He became a father after he had sat on the throne. Although he was 49, he was incredibly fond of debauchery. The doctors of the Palace wrote a guide book for him with the title 'The Sultan's Return to his Youth'. Today that book is kept at Murad Molla Library in Çarşamba. The book has three parts; The first part has a calendar on which his menu of every single hour of 365 days is shown. The second part 'tells about how a man can continue his potential at the peak. And the third part describes all the medicine empowering a man's action in sex. It seems that, Sultan Abdülhamid

The hanging with the imperial seal belongs to Selim III.

stuck to that recipe and had twenty-two children at the age of 49. Twelve of his children were girls and ten were boys.

Abdülhamid I had had Mustafa IV from Sineperver who later stayed in Harem for a year as the Sultana Mother during his son's reign. She got blind after her son had been dethroned. His another wife, Humaşah Sultana gave birth to Prince Mehmed. The only Sultana he was in love with, was Ruhşah. No Ottoman Sultan had ever loved a woman as much as he loved Ruhşah. In the archives of the Topkapı Palace we have some documents in his own handwriting stating how much he was in love with her. Ruhşah, on the other hand, would disdain most of the time. To the contrary of what is known, she might have been the only woman in the Ottoman's history who could have said 'no' to a Sultan when he had desired her. Despite the Sultan's wishes and requirements she was able to turn him down at times.

Abdülhamid, to make her come to be with him, would call out "My sweetheart, the owner of my heart, I could kiss your foot and even die for you".

In one of his letters kept in the archives of the Topkapı Palace;

"My sweetheart, please honour me tonight with your beautiful body. I would sacrifice myself for you. I had difficulty in holding myself last night, so, please my dear, do not torture me tonight. I do not have any patience anymore! Let me kiss your foot!".

An aigrette is pictured below.

It is understood that she would disdain at times. Even if the old Sultan was furious now and then, he would still pencil in more letters to her to reveal his desires in order to convince his unique Sultana;

" Madam! Do whatever you want with me; either kill or torture. I am surrendered. I am your prisoner. Please come tonight. (.......) I am pleading you to honour me tonight, if you don't, you may cause my death. I cannot hold myself anymore..."

It is understood that Ruhşah was indifferent to his pleading. That's why, in another letter, he would address to her;

".......If you don't come tonight I will understand that you do not love me. The situation I am in now, is unbearable ! Even my opponents feel sorry for me ! "

In another letter addressed to his great love;

"There is only you in my life who can put out this flame! , If you do not, who can? You will be the remedy to my misery"

In all his letters, still preserved in a very good condition, he reveals his love and his desires to be with her at nights;

"My Ruhşah! My sweetheart, my unique woman, I can sacrifice myself for you !"

He would reflect his sincere feelings to his letters. Those letters prove that, the affairs in the Harem were all accomplished by mutual consent.

Abdülhamid I got paralised and died at the

age of 65 in the year 1789 upon the Russians' annexation of Crimea in 1783 and the defeats against the Russians in 1787 and Austria in 1788. After his death, Ruhşah became an ordinary woman in the Harem. She later went to Mecca for pilgrimage by sake of the donations she had received from Abülhamid. She died in 1807 and was buried at Hamidiye sepulchre.

Abdülhamid I's mother Rabia Sermi Sultana had died long before her son completed his post as the Sultan. So, in the meantime, the Harem had been managed by one of the oldest women. Upon Abdülhamid's death, Selim III ascended to the throne. After he had sat on the throne, his mother Mihrişah Sultana became the authority as the Sultana Mother in the Harem. She moved into the Sultana Mother's chamber that had been unused for a long time, with a splendid parade.

The aigrettes worn on the head were always ornamented with emeralds, diamonds and brilliants. The aigrette in the picture belongs to II. Beyazıd.

Selim III, Mihrişah Sultana and the Concubine Mihriban

Mihrişah Sultana, a Georgian beauty, had been sent to the old palace upon her husband's death in 1774 but she later came back in the Harem as the Sultana Mother when her son Selim III. sat on the Ottoman throne.

Selim III. ascended to the throne at the age of 28 was fond of poetry, music and entertainment. He had a refined personality. Selim III has a place in history with his poems the lyrics which are even read and listened today. He used the nickname 'İlhami' in his poems. We would like to tell something about that interesting Sultan who used to be in close contact with the poets and the musicians of the time. He was a total reformer. He wanted to restructure all the bodies of the government since he thought Europe had considerably got more developed than the Ottomans at that time. He was aware of their underdevelopment and thought they were not able to catch up with them with the reforms taking place in the army only. He was in favour of a reform from head to foot. At that time, there started the revolution movement in France effecting all the thrones throughout Europe. All the thrones in Europe started to be terminated one after another. So, having been effected by that movement, Selim III started his reforms immediately. First of all, he formed a new army called 'Nizam-ı Cedid' in 1793 and terminated the Yeniçeri Ocağı (The old army, Janissaries). He thought the old army

A painting of Selim III by Konstantin from Kapıdağ, Topkapı Palace.
A painting illustrating Selim III horseback, Dolmabahçe Palace.

had been degenerated and completed its task. The new army was localised in two main barracks which had been built by his order before he started his reforms. The new barracks were in Selimiye(on the Anatolian side) and Levent (On the European side). The new army, unlike the previous one, was quite disciplined and very well trained. Besides, he opened a Navy School in Heybeliada(an island off coast of Istanbul). In order to grow scientists for the army, he started an Institute of Engineering. The members of the old army started to resist his reforms. Having been supported by those who had lost great benefits out of that, they were all against his restructuring work. In his spare time, Selim III used to compose music, recite poems and play the ney (Oriental flute). At that time, the palace was full of European poets, musicians and painters. He mad good friends with those.

He had two chambers constructed, one for himself and the other for his mother, Mihrişah Sultana. The walls of the Sultana Mother's chamber were covered with beautiful oriental pictures and wooden ornaments. The fireplace in the chamber would complete the showy decoration. His mother spent 18 years in that posh chamber during his son's sultanate.

She was very kindhearted and benevolent. She very much liked to invest her money in charity organisations and work. She had the

Imperial officials.

Mihrişah Sultan Mosque in Halıcıoğlu, the Mihrişah Valide Sultan fountain in Eminönü, and another fountain in Beşiktaş constructed. She also had many fountains and schools restored throughout the Empire. She got too sick during the last couple of years of her life. Her illness led her to death in 1805. She was buried at the sepulchre built for herself in Eyüp.

Selim III used to organise some concerts at the palace. On those nights new songs would introduced to the Sultan and the ones he particularly liked be performed by the oriental music group. His lyrics were admired by the very famous composer of the time, Hammamizade İsmail Efendi. In his era, there used to be some ballet shows at the palace. And, the palace was introduced to the piano and the harp as the first time in the Ottoman history by that same Sultan who was very open-minded and modern.

On one of those nights, all singers, composers and instrument players took place at the Sertab mansion. Ishak, one of the most famous musicians of the time was there, too. The music had already started when he arrived. The guards at the gate did not let him go in. At that very moment Selim III overheard the incident. He stood up, walked to the gate and shouted at the guardian "Look! Guardian, I can find one hundred thousand guardians like yourself but a great musician like İshak is not likely to be born once in a few hundred years. " So, this was a proof of his respect to the artists, musicians and poets. As he himself was a musician he could appreciate all the musicians and the artists, too.

Let me tell you one of his narratives relating to Sadullah Ağa. Sadullah Ağa was a well-known musician. Selim III would appreciate his music and respect him very much. He asked him to teach some of his concubines at that time. While teaching one of his concubines, he fell in love with one, named Mihriban. As the days passed, that became a mutual affection. He was in a weird situation, on one side there existed the Sultan's trust and respect to him, but on the other his love. That was an incredible dilemma for Sadullah Ağa. He was only able to declare his love with the songs he was teaching her as they were watched by one of the assistant masters according to the imperial traditions. He finally decided to talk to Mihriban face to face as he had already been prepared to die for her love. As they were closely monitored, that was risky, though. He took all the risks and openly declared his love to Mihriban who had been well aware of his affection long before. She responded positively.

The Sultan got very furious after he had learnt about his deception. According to the traditions, he had to be killed. He ordered his guardians to imprison him. But, as he was going to be killed by the Sultan's executioners, in rushed some of the Sultan's friends saying that the Sultan had forgiven him and that he had to be kept imprisoned. As a matter of fact, the Sultan hadn't ordered him to be kept in prison as they stated, but he had ordered him to be executed instead. While in prison, he still had Mihriban in his mind. In there, he continued his work and composed a new song called 'Bayati Araban' The ones around the Sultan decided to have the Sultan listen to his new song on one of the days that he was going to be in the mood. It was another night full of music at the palace and the Sultan had already been seated in his place. Selim III let the music begin. Then, the oriental orchestra started to play Sadullah Ağa's new song. Everybody's eyes were on the Sultan who seemed to have been delighted with the song he had never heard before. When the song was over, you could have heard a pin drop. They were all waiting for his reaction. The Sultan, looking around, asked "Whose song is it?" Everyone's eyes were on the carpet. Some could only whisper his name "Sadullah Ağa ! He had composed it before he died but never had the chance to have the orchestra play that in his lifetime." He suddenly felt so miserable, tears came into his eyes. He was about to weep. He started to spank his lap with his hands for he had ordered him to be killed. He started to

Sarıklar Ağa, one of the imperial officials.

The celebration ceremony of Selim III. The officials of the Palace would line up to celebrate the Bayram(Religious feast) of the Sultan. He would receive the people on his throne placed outside the Ak Ağalar gate.

125

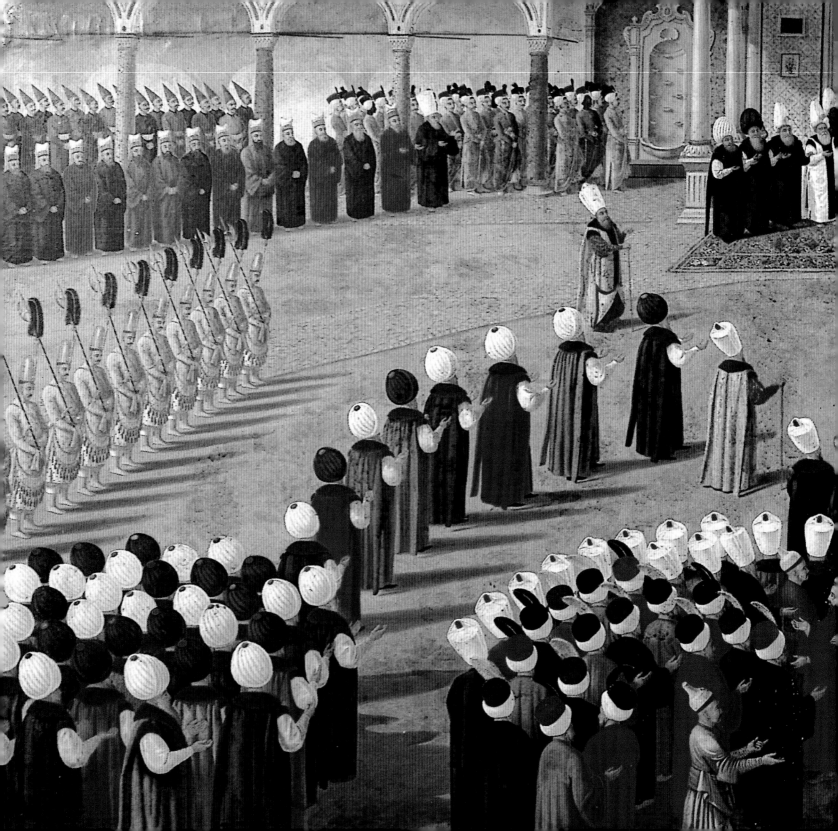

show his grief by the words he performed " How did I order a great composer to be killed !" Their Sultan's grief upset all the people in the hall, too. Some of his men could not stand the incident any longer and said "His Majesty, Sadullah Ağa is alive !" And, taking all the risks into consideration, he explained what they had done to save his life. The reaction of Selim III

A miniature illustrating Selim III with his father during his service as a prince.

relieved everybody there. He did not get angry, instead, he was incredibly happy to hear that he was still alive. He immediately ordered him to be brought in the hall. He was in the hall in the next couple of minutes, quite perplexed, a little shy. He had been beaten by his love to Mihriban ignoring all the imperial traditions. A concubine's honour was the Sultan's honour according to the imperial traditions. Sadullah Ağa was there, standing with his eyes on the floor in front of the Sultan. The Sultan forgave him of what he had done and said "Not even one but let all my concubines be yours with pleasure." Selim III exhibited his greatness and gave Ssadullah Ağa a lot of presents and married him to Mihriban.

The Sultan who was a poet and a composer at the same time, would spend his nights in the great hall listening to music and the days by following up the reforms he had started. Some people who were against his reforms had already started to criticise him saying he was after foreigners and that he was trying to adapt a new system which the European were in. They were also trying to provoke the people against him.

Meanwhile, Selim III married his uncle Abdülhamid's daughter Esma Sultana to one of his admirals, Kaptanı-ı Derya Hüseyin Pasha. She had been married for 11 years when his husband died. She was then a 25-year-old widow. Never remarried again and led a colourful life of the richest widow in Istanbul. With her mother, Sineperver Sultana, it was that Esma Sultana who had played an important role in the Kabakçı rebellion in order to have his brother Mustafa IV ascend to the throne. With their provocation, the soldiers of the previous army (Janissaries) and the ones against his reforms rebelled on 29th. May, 1807. They were led by Kabakçı Mustafa Çavuş. That's why it has always been remembered as the Kabakçı rebellion. The rebels attacked the Şeyh-ül İslam's (The head of the Ottoman Muslims) mansion at the At Square and asked for his formal declaration to dethrone Selim III. He had to give them that declaration. The rebels submitted Selim III the declaration of his dethronement signed by Şeyh-ül İslam. He very calmly said "I wish Mustafa IV good luck on the throne" So, his Sultanate which had lasted for 18 years came to an end. He was only 46 years old then. Having been accompanied by his two women he secluded himself in one of the chambers at the palace called 'the cage'. His misery in that cage had lasted only for a year and two months when the Ruscuk Senator Alemdar Mustafa Pasha attacked the palace with his 20.000 men to make Selim III sit on the Ottoman throne again. His army camped right outside the Topkapı Palace. He ordered his soldiers to imprison the Sultan and sent in

Şeyh-ül İslam to have Selim III ascend to the throne. In the mean time, Mustafa's supporters had already convinced him to kill Selim III and Mahmud II immediately if he wanted to continue his Sultanate. And, he ordered Selim III and Mahmud II to be executed.

A portrait of Selim III by Zonaro.

The portrait of Mahmud II on the Yıldız Porcelain plate. Beside his portrait, Nusretiye Mosque and Mahmudiye battle ship are also illustrated.

A Brave Woman In The Harem; Cevri Kalfa

To accomplish the Sultan's order to kill Selim III and Prince Mahmud, The Treasurer Master Ebe Selim, The Head Foot Equerry Gürcü Abdül Fettah, The Deputy Treasurer Zcnci Nezir, Mirahur Kör Mehmed and some other men rushed into the Harem. They were walking through the corridors, but they had difficulty in finding their way as they had never been there before. It was impossible for them to reach the place where Selim III was. A while later, Peykidil, one of Mustafa IV's Cariyes showed them the way to Selim III's room. All of them hurried into the room. Sultan Selim had already understood that the newcomers were not friendly. He called out "Are you the executioners?." Zenci Nezir was shouting at the ones with him "Why are you standing there? while Pakize Kadın was crying out "Please do not kill his Majesty !" Blood was dripping off her hands as she tried to hold a sword pointing at the Sultan. They threw her to a corner. But, at that very moment, it was Refet Kadın who was trying to defend him. They threw her away, too. Sultan Selim had nothing on the hand but his ney (Kind of Flute) to help him defend himself. He neither wanted to go into any disputes nor

liked fights. He was a musician and a poet, he was not a quarrelsome person unlike many other Sultans who had reigned the Ottomans for hundreds of years. He was not afraid of death

A painting of Abdülmecid, the son of Mahmud II.

131

and that's why he was not doing anything to defend himself. With his pride, he was just sitting there looking down the executioners and reciting the Islamic formula "God is great". In that very moment a sword divided his head in

The Golden path where Cevri Kalfa fought to save the life of Mahmud II, was tiled with the İznik chinaware belonging to the 17th. century before.

half. Strokes followed one another. The dead body of the great Sultan of a time was lying on the ground. While Refet Kadın was crying having embraced his dead body Bostancı Hacı Ali threw her away. The songs and the neys stopped. The Harem which had been full of musical notes once, was silent then. You could have heard a pin drop. The executioners left his corpse outside the Harem. As Selim III had no children, the only heir was prince Mahmud, Abdülhamid I's son from Nakşidil. The executioners were not done yet so they started to look for him. In order to keep Mustafa IV on the throne, he had to be executed too. They were running along the corridors of the Harem with their swords on hands. Concubine Peykidil was leading them to their new target. Meanwhile, some eunuchs of the Harem, Kasım Ağa, İsa Ağa and Amber Ağa having heard that the executioners had arrived in the Harem to kill Selim III rushed into his chamber. But, when they realised that he had already been killed they immediately hurried to prince Mahmud's chamber in order to save his life, at least. The Prince was not in his chamber as Cevri Kalfa had hidden him in her own chamber. So, those eunuchs made their way to her chamber which was on the 'Golden corridor' where the Sultans used to give away golden liras to Concubines once. It was 46 metres long and 4 metres wide. Cevri Kalfa and prince Mahmud were just outside the gate of her chamber. There were 50 stairs to access the chamber. The executioners arrived there, too. The eunuchs were downstairs covering the stairway. The executioners were larger in number though. The court outside the door to the chamber was being defended by Kasım Ağa. He was fighting bravely and was able to stop them there for a while. But, a dagger thrown by one of those executioners wounded him. Having seen that, Cevriye Kalfa started to throw ashes onto them from her brazier. They had to be stopped somehow, or at least, delayed to let the prince run away. All she was trying to do was to let the prince escape onto the roof through the chimney. She yelled out at Hafız İsa and Amber Ağa "Help him climb up to the roof !". She was knocked out by those who had rushed into the room. Prince Mahmud was about the leave the room through the chimney when a dagger hit him in the arm, but it did not stop him reach on the roof. He was able to climb up the roof. Amber and Hafız Ağa were by the chimney and trying to keep them away from there. At that very moment, the news of Alemdar's soldiers arrival at the palace struck the executioners as a lightning. As they heard the sound of their feet, they were well aware of their presence nearby. They stopped the fight, retreated and started to run away down the stairs. As Alemdar Mustafa Pasha was proceeding his way in the Harem, he met the dead body of Selim III. He stopped, knelt down and started to cry out "His Majesty, I have come all the way from my province to save you but it is more than poignant to see your dead body

Another panel made of china belongs to the 17th. century.

133

here!. It is high time I terminated all those who had done this to you in this damn Palace now?" It wasn't long before one of his men called out "Come on Pasha it is not the time to cry now, we have to save the life of the Prince at least!". So, burying his grief inside, he ordered "Find him immediately". His men went away to search for him. Finally, as they saw the prince on the roof, they helped him down. After his clothes had been cleaned, he was taken to the Pasha who said "I have come here to have your uncle sit on the throne but it is understood that it has been your destiny to ascend to the throne". So, he was declared the new Sultan. And there, after being declared as the Sultan, Mahmud II appointed Alemdar Mustafa Pasha as his Grand Vizier.

Alemdar Mustafa Pasha was a brave man, everyone knew that the ones who had been involved in the massacre wouldn't be able to get along with that. He took his revenge by having all those, who had got involved in the murder, killed one by one within time. Of course, he was not oblivious of Peykidil either. She was strangled to death and thrown into the sea. Alemdar Mustafa Pasha died by igniting all gunpowder barrels when the ones who had been hatred of him set his villa on fire. So, he committed suicide as a hero and killed all those who had set him a trap with himself. Cevriye

The inside of the sultanate boats were ornamanted with mother-of -pearl.

The Dolmabahçe Palace was built by Abdülmecid and the Harem was relocated there afterwards. Abdülmecid is illustrated on his boat.

Kalfa passed a comfortable life with the donations of the Sultan and invested most of her money in charitable societies and establishments. She died in 1804. Refet Kadın whose husband had been murdered in front of her eyes lived until the age of 90. Mahmud II, after sitting on the throne at the age of 23, governed his country for 31 years. During his service, he tried to do his best in catching up with the European civilisation and continued the reforms especially in the clothing of his public and the state affairs. The reflection of his reforms soon started to be seen on the public. As he had been well-educated by sake of his uncle Selim III, he was very cultured and modern. His uncle wanted him to be raised at the European standards. He could play the ney and the tambur (six-stringed lute) as well. At the same time, he was a composer and a poet like his uncle.

His mother Nakşidil Sultana who was of the French originality effected him in his reforms in many ways. Nakşidil Sultana who had entered the Harem as a Concubine was able rise to the rank of the Sultana Mother on his son's accession to the throne. Nakşidil Sultana, whom we narrated about in the 'The Favourites' section died in 1817 after a service of 9 years as the Sultana Mother.

The end of The Dynasty

Mahmud II reigned his country for 31 years which was quite a long time. During his long sultanate since he preferred to stay in the palaces by the Bosphorus , Topkapı Palace lost its distinction. Upon Mahmud II's death, his 16-year-old son Abdülmecid ascended to the throne and his mother Bezmialem Sultana became the Sultana Mother. She was the last Sultana Mother who lived and died at the Topkapı Palace. Her death caused a deep sorrow for the public as much as her son Abdülmecid. To her memory, he had the Valide Sultan Mosque built by the Dolmabahçe Palace which had recently been built by himself, too.

Upon completion of the Dolmabahçe Palace in 1856 the construction of which had started in 1843, he moved to that new Palace with his Harem leaving the old Palace unattended. He used to visit Küçüksu and Ihlamur mansion houses that he had them built before, quite often. Sultan Abdülmecid had a son named Sultan Reşad from Gülcemal, Abdülhamid II from his second wife Tirimüjgan and Murad V from Şevkefze Kadın.

Abdülaziz sat on the Ottoman throne after he had died in 1861. Abdülaziz was not so fond of women as much as his father and brother had been. He was well-built and had an athletic body. He continued the construction facilities his brother had started and had the Beylerbeyi and the Çırağan Palaces built. His mother Pertevniyal Sultana became the Sultana

The blue hall and the gate of the Treasury at the Dolmabahçe Palace built by Abdülmecid.

Mother and continued charity work, too.

Upon Abdülaziz's dethronement and death Murad V. ascended to the throne which lasted for only 93 days. He was said to have been inefficient on the throne and dethroned afterwards. He was obliged to move to the Çırağan Palace and live there with his wife and the children.

Abdülhamid, who was 34 at that time, ascended to the throne. As his mother had died long before, his step mother Perustu Kadın became the Sultana Mother. Although she was the head of the Harem, she never interfered in anybody's business and passed her time with charity work.

Abdülhamid II having moved to the Yıldız Palace, ruled his country for 33 years from there. He was sent to Thessalonika in 1909

The Çırağan Palace which was built by Sultan Abdülaziz between 1863 and 1871 had to host Murad V compulsorily after his reign of 93 days. It was burnt down in 1910 and restored afterwards.

after being dethroned. He was later accommodated in the Beylerbeyi Palace and lived there until the end of his life. Mehmed Reşad, the son of Abdülmecid from Gülcemal Sultana, ascended to the throne at the age of 65. He immediately had the Dolmabahçe Palace that had been untouched for the past 33 years, restored and moved there. Since Gülcemal Sultana had died in Sultan Reşad's childhood, the Harem had no Sultana Mother at his time. That old Sultan was able to rule his country for 9 years until his death in 1918. His son Mehmed Vahideddin ascended to the Ottoman throne as the last Sultan in the Imperial history. It is recorded that he officially married his 4 wives.

During Mehmed Vahideddin's sultanate the first world war was in progress. The Ottomans were the allies of the Germans in the war, and as they had been beaten, the Ottomans were

also declared defeated by the occupation forces and their lands were invaded by them.

Turks started their war of independence in the leadership of Mustafa Kemal Atatürk with the slogan of 'Either independence or death !' and defeated all the occupation forces all over Anatolia. Meanwhile, the pro-English Sultan Vahideddin took an English ship at the Dolmabahçe Palace and left the country. So, the Ottoman throne had been left unattended and the young Turkish Republic was founded in its place.

Upon the termination of the Sultanate, the Republic was founded and Caliphate was ended on 3 March 1924. So, with the last Caliph, Abdülmecid Efendi, the Dynasty and an era came to end. Today, we have some books written by the grandchildren of the last Ottoman Sultans enlightening their era and the Harem of the time.

Abdülhamid II reigned his country from the Yıldız Palace for 33 years. Yıldız Palace consists of many mansion houses built on different dates. The ceremonial hall is illustrated below at the Şale Mansion House.

Walking About The Harem

Sultan Mehmed the Conqueror had a Palace built in Bayezıd Square after he had taken Istanbul in 1453, but as it got too small for the growing population of the Palace within time he had to have today's Topkapı Palace built between 1472 and 1478. The Harem, the first compounds of which had been constructed by Sultan Mehmed, continued its expansion until the era of Murad III who had it restored and completely moved the old Harem to the new Palace. His successors carried on the expansion work in the Harem which grew steadily with the new compounds having been added within time.

Now, let us start our tour of the Harem which kept its mystery for 300 years and never felt the presence of any other men's feet but the Sultans only.

Dome with Sideboards:

The Harem which is under the Adalet Tower is accessible from the Arabalar Gate. As the women of the Harem would get on horse-drawn carriages at that gate, it was called the Arabalar (Carriages) Gate. It has another gate opening into the third courtyard called Kuşhane which is used as the exit gate for the visitors. As you walk in through the Arabalar Gate which bears an inscription belonging to Murad III dated 1587, you arrive in the main hall where all external services of the Harem were undertaken once. This place is called the dome with sideboards as it has closets on all its

Another view from Topkapı Palace which reminds you of a big village.

walls. There comes Şadırvanlı Sofa after this square hall with a dome on the top. This place is separated with rectangular girdle. The first part is covered with a vault and the second one left plain. As there used to be a fountain there

The dome with a vault is at the entrance of the harem.

once, it is known as Şadırvanlı Taşlık (Courtyard with a fountain). That fountain now exists in the pool of Murad III's chamber. The walls of this 20x8 width courtyard are adorned with the 17th. century china. In the medallions, the china on the walls have, the names of the ten people the Prophet Mohammed promised the Heaven, bear. Besides, there stands an inscription bearing information on the restoration of the Harem by Mehmed IV after the 1665 fire. To the left of this place there is another inscription on the Meşkhane Gate bearing some verse from the Koran dated 1668. The Adalet tower is accessible by some stairs from the door to the right of Şadırvanlı Sofa. On top of that door, there bears "One hour long equitable action is much more precious than a purposeless pray of seventy years". The Ottoman Sultans would monitor their Grand Viziers' dates from a window of that Adalet Tower.

The Masjid (Small Mosque) of the Eunuchs:

Walking past the the Şadırvanlı Taşlık, you arrive in a square hall where the eunuchs used to perform their prayers. This hall is located before the door with an inscription on the top. It is thought that this place was restored after the 1665 fire. The walls of the hall are adorned with china of XVIIth. century. We can see calligraphic art on the ceiling and the picture

Plan of The Harem

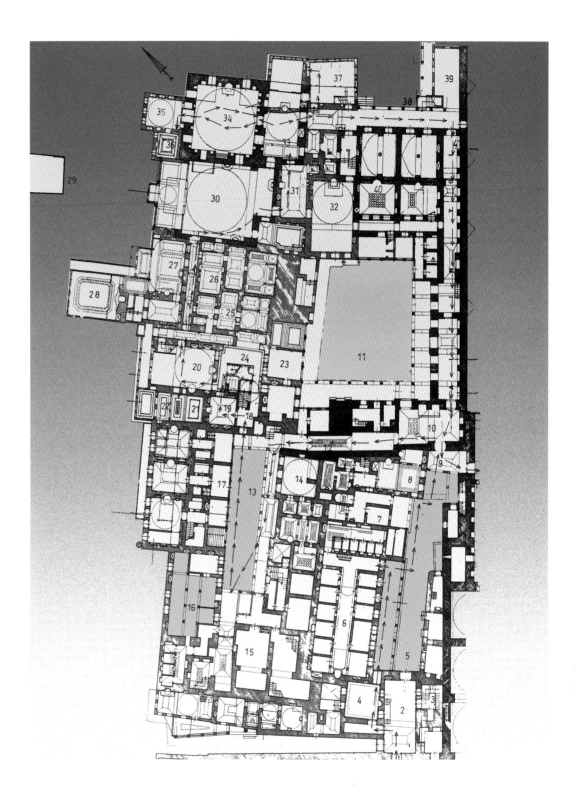

The china with Kaaba motifs on is in the niche of the small mosque belonging to the black eunuchs.

of the Caaba on the niche. The side walls have the pictures of Medina and Arafat (holy places in Saudi Arabia) in light green. Through the gate across the niche you can reach the Assisstant-Master school where the cariyes used to be tutored. Right across that and by the Adalet tower the chamber of the chamberlain is located. The chamberlains, treasurer master and the Sultans' dwarf clowns used to live in there.

The ward of the Eunuchs:

The eunuchs also called "The black Footmen", as known, would be castrated in childhood and taken in the Harem to safeguard it. They were supervised by the Darüs-saade Ağası (The Head Eunuch) or Kızlar Ağası (The Head Eunuch responsible for the Girls). The three-storey eunuchs' ward is located by the eunuchs' courtyard. It has rooms on both sides along its corridors. The first floor has a bedroom, Selamlık (room for the men) a guest room and the oom for the assistant head eunuch responsible for the gate, Başkapı Gulamı Ağa. The rooms located on the right hand side are the cellars.

The second floor has some wards belonging to the middle class eunuchs, and the third floor which was added on the building in the 18th. century, belonged to the novice eunuchs. All those rooms are adorned with china.

There is a fireplace across the corridor the left side of which is adorned with 17th. century china. Stairs, lead you upstairs from there. Beneath the stairs you can access the chamber of Kızlar ağası and the restroom for the eunuchs.

The Chamber of
Darüs-Saade Ağası (Head Eunuch):

The Kızlar Ağası chamber is located to the left of the eunuchs' courtyard. The eunuchs received in the Harem as a novice, would promote to the ranks of Ortanca (middle), Haslılar (Specials), Yayla Başı Gulamı (Tableland head) and Başkapı Gulamı (The eunuch responsible for the main gate). Their top rank would be the Head Eunuch. The Head Eunuchs would come the third in the protocol line after the Grand Vizier and the Şeyh-ül İslam. The chamber of the Head Eunuch has such a location that its windows overlook the Harem gates. They could easily monitor the entrance to the Harem.

The entrance hall of the Head Eunuchs' chamber is in a vast niche. The entrance, the walls of its rooms and the fireplace are adorned with 17th. century china. It has a Turkish bath, too. The building has two floors. Şehzadeler Okulu (The school for the Ottoman Princes) is on the second floor.

Şehzadeler Okulu
(The School for the Princes):

The Ottoman Princes would be tutored there. The walls along the stairs leading you upstairs are covered with the European china and adorned with plant motifs. It has two sections. The first section is rectangular shaped and quite large with a plain ceiling. Its walls have china bearing some Caaba pictures. A baroque style marble fireplace is mounted on the wall. The book shelves on the walls and the niches are adorned with rococo gilding gold. The upper parts of the walls have some china belonging to the 17th. century bearing

The small mosque, the walls of which are covered with the china of the 17th. century, has some Kaaba and Arafat figures on its side walls too.

149

cypress figures and some Islamic verses. The signature under the inscription above the shelves prove that it was written by the Head Eunuch Beşir Ağa in 1749. The bronze brazier and the two candlestick in the hall are of the empiric style.

Some view from the eunuchs' courtyard. The courtyard has a small mosque for the eunuchs on the side.

The Main Entrance Gate to the Harem:

To the east of the Eunuch's courtyard which is 60 metres in length and 8-10 metres in width lies the main entrance gate to the Harem. Today's exit gate Kuşhane kapısı lies to the left of this main gate.

On top of the gate, there is an inscription bearing some verse from the Koran telling about the manners on how to enter homes. As you walk in through the main gate made of iron, there is a courtyard with big mirrors on walls where the eunuchs used to stand on duty all the time. This was the crucial point as they, themselves, would never get in and let anybody in either. The sections inside were all in control of assistant masters. There are three doors in there. The one on the very left leads you to the corridor of Cariyes' chamber, the one in the middle to the Sultana Mother courtyard and the other to the Golden Path which is 46 metres long and 4 metres wide.

This door was used by the Sultans and the Princes. The Sultan after girding on a sword would return back to the Harem with a glorious parade. After saddling down his horse at the Sultana Mother courtyard, he would follow the route along the golden road to his throne. It was traditional for him to deliver golden coins at the Concubines waiting for their Sultan on both sides of that Golden Path. The door in the middle opens into the Sultana Mother courtyard. Around this courtyard, the Sultana

Mother chamber and the chamber for the sergeants-at-arms are located. The Sultana Mothers, Sergeants-at-arms, The Favourites and the Felicities would reach their chambers by using that door.

A view of the Harem gate from the head eunuch's chamber.

The Concubines' Courtyard:

The door on the left is the one used by the women not belonging to the Sultans' family, the Concubines, the Masters and the Assistant Masters. By iron sliding bars, those doors would be kept locked from inside by the Concubines and even the eunuchs were never let in. Now, to be able to reach the Concubines or in another words, Kadın Efendis courtyard, we should go through this door. There is an inscription on top that door bearing "Our God, who is able to open all gates, please open us some lucky gates too!" should be reflecting their wishes.

After we have walked in, we come across some stone benches to the left of the corridor. The eunuchs would put the trays, on which they used to carry the meals, on those benches and close the door. Then, the door at the rear end of the corridor would open and some Concubines would come to collect the tray. The Concubines' courtyard is accessible from the end of the passage. This part was constructed in 16th. century.

This courtyard with porches on three sides has a fountain, a large domed bath, the entrance door of the stairs to the chamber of the assistant masters. Across that, the kitchen, cellar, laundrette and the toilets and next to it, the Kadınefendiler's chamber and the Concubines' wards are located.

152

The Concubines' Ward:

The door by the Kadınefendiler chamber opens onto the stairs called 'forty stairs'. The fifth door beside it, is the Concubines' ward where about 25 Concubines would live in. Inside has two separated sections. Its windows overlook the courtyard and has a mezzanine supported by marble pillars. The pillar gaps were closed by wooden separators and new sections formed upon the growth of the Concubines' population in the Harem.

The novice Concubines would stay on the ground and the experienced ones on the upper floor. One old Concubine would stay in a ward of every ten Concubines. They would clear away their room in the daytime and make their beds to sleep at night. The fireplace on the ground floor would heat all the chamber. The Concubines would inspect the novice Concubines and they, themselves were inspected by the Assistant Masters. Of course, the Masters would inspect their Assistants, too.

The forty step stairs by the Kadınefendiler chamber would lead down to the Harem hospital. In fact, the total number of steps is 52. By the end of the stairs there lies the Sultana Mother cellar. Since the the Concubines' ward lies to the East of this courtyard, it is, therefore called Concubines' courtyard. You can see the Patients' Master's room by that ward. There are two sections here; one of them is the Hospital's bath and the other, Hospital's kitchen. Across the courtyard there lies a laundrette and a place they used to wash the dead bodies. The ones died in the Harem would be washed there and taken out by the Meyit door.

The courtyard where the hospital was located in. One needs to take forty steps down the stairs to reach the hospital.

The Chamber of Kadınefendis (Sultans' Wives):

To the right of the courtyard, the chambers belonging to the second, third and the fourth are located. The first, so called the head Kadınefendi chamber would lie in the Valide

Sultana courtyard by the hall with a fireplace. As known, the wives of the Sultans were called Kadınefendis and they were ranked as, the first, the second etc.. The second Kadınefendi chamber has a wooden door and very low divans. It has two rooms and the walls of which are covered with Kütahya china. The china on the walls have been repaired within time. From there, you enter a narrow corridor. The toilet is located on the right hand side and the stairs to the opposite. That corridor takes you to the main room. On the wall to the right there are some shelves, a fireplace and a sink with cold and hot water taps. On the opposite wall the windows remind you of flower bouquets. The fireplace has been refurbished. The room is adorned with a copper brazier in the middle and divans covered with silk fabric. The room to the left with small closets in was used to keep their beds and stuff. The bedrooms are located upstairs belonged to the Kadınefendis. The ceiling of the small room is plain. The main room has a domed ceiling adorned with calligraphic art. It is thought that those rooms which had been built for Kadınefendis were later used by the Assistant Masters of the Harem.

The Chamber of The Sultana Mother :

You can reach the Chamber of the Sultana Mother by the Kadınefendis' Chamber. Upon their sons' sitting on the throne, they would come to the Harem with a glorious parade and settle in that chamber. It was natural for them to keep so many Concubines and maids since they were the head of the Harem.

By walking past two tiny galleries you can reach the Sultana Mothers' Chamber. There lies a vast courtyard right outside the chamber. The entrance to the chamber is located in that courtyard. Now, we will get to know this courtyard and continue our tour in the chamber.

The courtyard is in open air. This courtyard is the core of the whole compounds as all other compounds rose around it. The golden road which is thought to have been built at the time of Sultan Mehmed, lies to the South and the wards belonging to the Masters and Assistant Masters of the Harem to the West of this courtyard.

The Pharmacy of the Harem is located next to them. The buildings to the East of The Sultana Mother's chamber, near the golden road belonged to Haseki Sultans. Kadınefendis, the wives of the Sultans after giving birth to baby sons were called 'Haseki Sultan'. The rooms used for births stand next to those compounds. On the other side of those compounds you can see the hall with a fireplace.

Hasekiler compound is accessible by a door in that hall. This chamber which is thought to have been built at the time of Sultan Mehmed, has a big hall with a fireplace a pavilion. Hürrem Sultana is said to have used this chamber as the first time. Later, those pavilions were covered and new compounds added to the building.

Çeşmeli Sofa (The hall with a fountain) is also accessible by a door from the same yard. Since the Sultans used to saddle down their

Prayers room opposite the bedroom of the Sultana Mother. It is separated from the bedroom by two bronze windows and a door. One wall is covered with china bearing the Kaaba motifs on.

The bedroom adorned with china at the Sultana Mother chamber.

The sitting hall of the Sultana Mother adorned with handmade motifs.

horses there after girding on a sword, it is therefore called 'The gate of the Throne', too. In there, the Sultans would also farewell their mothers while leaving for a war and ride on their horses in their armour.

By walking past two tiny galleries by the Kadınefedis chamber, you can reach the Sultana Mothers' Chamber. The first room to be seen at the entrance belonged to the head maid of the Sultana Mother. It is adorned with a brazier, china on its walls, inset cupboards covered with nacres. The Sultana Mother Chamber is accessible from there. The main entrance of the Sultana Mother's chamber is in the Sultana Mother courtyard. There lie two rooms the first of which was used as the waiting room for the incoming guests and the other was the entrance. The stairs opposite where the guards used to stand on duty lead you to the rooms upstairs. The Felicities and the Favourites who had passed the night with the Sultan used to stay in those three rooms. The top of its door bears an inscription dated 1667, which was two years after the 1665 fire. By that door you can reach the vast dining hall of the Sultana Mother's chamber. The hall has two floors. The first floor is covered with 17th. century china. The ornaments on the upper floor and on the dome were structured by Mahmud II in 1817. The dome is adorned with vine leaves and grapes. There is also a fireplace in there and the side of the window should have been used as the dining room.

The bedroom is accessible by a wooden gate to the left of this dining hall adorned with nacres. Its walls are covered with 17th. century

china and above is the wagon headed mirrors. There lies the bed covered with a curtain to the left. The Sultana Mother's pray room is connected to this bedroom by a door and a two windows made of bronze. The picture of Mecca dated 1667, is seen on its walls in light green.

The Sultana Mother's chamber restored many times between 16th and 20th. centuries and therefore has lost its originality. Its dome was repaired around the end of 18th. century and ornamented with the figures reflecting that era. The fireplace in there was the last place to

have been repaired. The fireplace was restored with the china from the Cevri Kalfa era. The Concubines under the control of the Sultana Mother would stay on the ground floor. By taking a look at the Sultan Mother Chamber from the courtyard you can see all three floors.

Now, let us tell you about the Selim III and the Mihrişah Sultana's chambers.

The Chamber of Mihrişah Sultana:

The top floor of the Sultana Mother's chamber belonged to the mother of Selim III,

Selim III had two chambers built reflecting the beauty of the Ottoman rococo. The closet of Selim III.

Mihrişah Sultana. It is accessible by some stairs on the side. Along those stairs you can see some landscape figures drawn under the western effect.

Upon her son's sitting on the throne Mihrişah Sultana moved in that chamber with a glorious parade. The architect of the Palace Melling constructed that chamber by Selim

The Chamber of Selim III by the Abdülhamid I Chamber reflects the beautiful samples of the Ottoman rococo. Various illustrations of the Selim III Chamber.

III's order for his mother, Mihrişah Sultana. Later, Selim III, after having been dethroned, had the chamber converted to a hidden section in which he lived for a about a year with his mother. The chamber is square in shape with a flat ceiling . It has two rooms. The ceilings of the both rooms are adorned with baroque, golden gilded rococo style ornaments. In the interior room is a marble, baroque style fireplace adorned with European tiles. On both sides of the fireplace you can see landscape pictures under the western effect. In the second room, the sides and the top of the window in a vast niche are adorned with the same kind of pictures.

The Chamber of Abdülhamid I :

The bedroom of Abdülhamid I is located by the Sultana Mother's Chamber opposite the Sultan's Hamam (Bath). The Ottoman Sultans would spend their nights at the Murad II Mansion until the era of Osman III (1754-1757). This part designed by the head architect Davut Ağa was used after having been adorned with rococo style ornaments by Osman II And Abdülhamid I. The Sultans after Osman III also used the room as their bedroom. But, since Abdülhamid had it restored, it has always been remembered after his name.

This place is rectangular in shape and has three covered sections. The walls and the ceilings are all adorned with baroque, golden

gilded rococo style ornaments. The chamber has a baroque style fountain covered with golden gilded pink and blue European tiles. You can access to the Selim III and Mihrişah Sultana Chambers from here.

Selim III's Love Chamber:

Selim III's Love chamber is accessible from the Abdülhamid I.'s bedroom. It is known that it had been built by Osman III. after having been restored by Selim III used by himself as his Love chamber. The chamber consists of two rooms called Selim III room and Selim III Love room. The chamber was built in 1790. It has wooden ceiling and is in a square shape. The ceilings and the walls of the both rooms are adorned with baroque, golden gilded rococo style ornaments. There is a marble fireplace in the chamber which reflects one of the best examples of the Turkish rococo style. The fireplace has white tiles in the interior part and blue flower patterned tiles on top of it.

The Mansion of Osman III :

A long narrow corridor connects Selim III chamber to Osman III Mansion. It was started to be constructed at the time of Mahmud I but completed by Osman III in 1754. The vine outside the Sultans' Courtyard is found on the interior fortress of the palace overlooking the Golden Horn.

The mansion which has a flat courtyard in the front consists of three rooms in one another. The walls are adorned with rococo and baroque style ornaments. Among those ornaments you can see brown and blue patterned European china. Besides, some pictures related to the life of the interior palace, under the European effect are found in the niche located in the middle room. The vast room is the richest room of the chamber.

The Sultans' and the Sultana Mothers' Baths:

As you walk towards the Hünkar Sofası from the Sultana Mother's chamber, the Sultans' and the Sultana Mothers' baths are found on the

Hünkar Sofası, the ceremonial hall of the Harem was built in 1585 and restored twice during Mehmed IV's sultanate and in the 18th. century.

right hand side. The most beautiful hamam in the Harem is the Sultan's bath which was constructed by Mimar Sinan in 16th. century with white marbles. Beside that is the Sultana Mothers' hamam which was restored by Turhan Sultana, the mother of Mehmed IV. It has the same plan as the Sultan's hamam. The both hamams' being located next to one another, made it easy to heat both of them by one stoke hole. The Sultan's hamam consists of three separate sections. The first section was used as the massaging and relaxation room. It is understood by the stains remained on walls that, there was some calligraphic art on them. There lie some wooden divans with white covers. The changing room has a gilded wooden closet and a crystal mirror framed in golden gilding.

The third section has the main bath. The hot part of the hamam is accessible through the cold part. It is illuminated through some small and big round windows on the dome. The iron caged part to the left was the place where the Sultans washed. That part was all covered with iron bars to protect the Sultans from being assassinated. As we leave this place with elegant taps and small cabins, we can reach the most glorious hall of the Palace, The Hünkar Sofası.

The Hünkar Sofası :

Hünkar Sofası was the hall where the Sultans would receive their guests and spend

Some parts of Hünkar Sofası were adorned with the Delf china during restoration work in the 18th. century..

The china on the throne bears the name of Mehmed IV and the date of 1666.

their daytime. Hünkar Sofası was built under the supervision of the architect Davud Ağa in 1585 a little after the Murad III Mansion. This domed hall was completely restored by the end of 18th. century by Mehmed IV after the fire of 1665. Osman III had the balcony and the divans under that built and later, it was started to be used as the ceremonial hall. Including the ones on the top, it has 26 windows in total. The dome rises on four sharp-pointed belts adorned with rococo style. The wooden parts of the dome like the windows and the closets are ornamented with various designs. The 16th. century original decoration of the belts give us an idea on the architectural style of the mentioned century. Hünkar Sofası covered

with the blue patterned Delf china on a white ground has a throne opposite the entrance where the Sultan used to sit on. Large Chinese vases are placed on both sides of the throne. There lie oriental sofas covered with

velvet to the left of the throne. The balcony above was the place where the orchestra used to play music. The clocks placed symmetrically were the presents of the Queen Victoria. The wooden armchair in another corner was the present of the German Emperor Wilhelm II for Abdülhamid II. The closet covered with a mirror in the left corner of the hall is, in fact, a door. The Sultans could pass to the other parts of the Harem through that hidden door. On the china, the walls have all around the hall, is a verse from the Koran "Ayet-ül Kürsi". The part above the throne bears the date of the restoration work in 1666 and the name of Sultan Murad IV who had it done at the time. The interior part of the sharp-pointed belts and the pendentives are adorned with the 16th. century calligraphic art. During restoration work, the original style was able to be kept.

The Çeşmeli Sofa
(The Courtyard with a Fountain):

To be able to arrive at Murad III's mansion from Hünkar Sofası you should walk through the Çeşmeli Sofa. It was the gallery where the princes and Kadınefendis used wait outside to enter the Sultan's chamber. As it has a fountain on of its walls it has always been called "The Çeşmeli Sofa" which is rectangular in shape. The name of the Sultan Mehmed IV

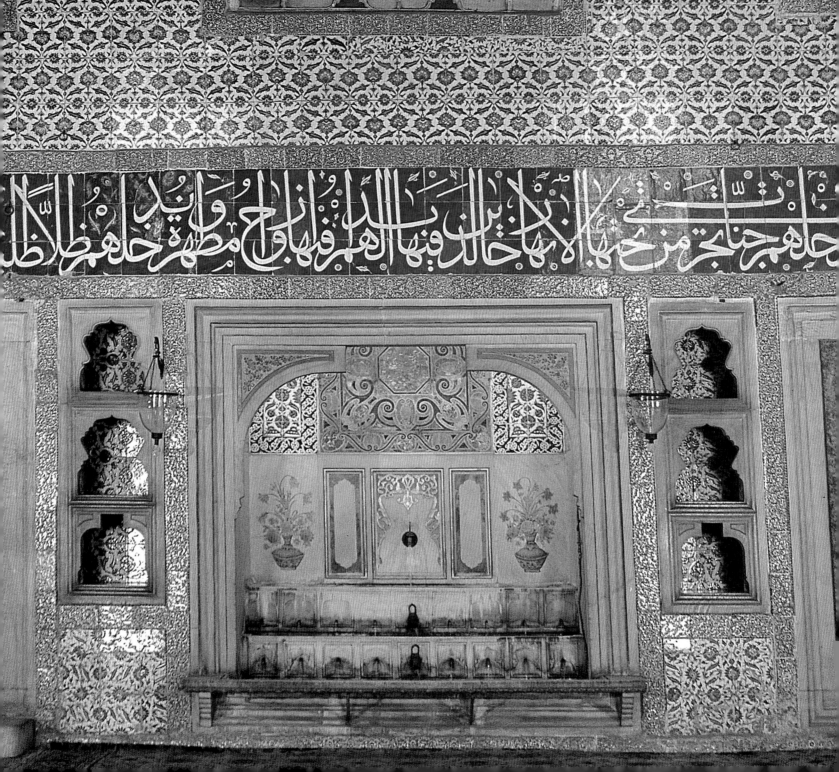

can be read on that fountain. This vast hall the walls of which are covered with 17th. century china opens into the Ocaklı Sofa. Ocaklı Sofa has a door leading onto the Sultana Mother

courtyard. This gate was also used by the Sultans so therefore it is called Taht Kapısı. The Sultans would reach Ocaklı Sofa and walking past Çeşmeli Sofa they could get in their chamber. The walls of this place with a vast fireplace are adorned with 17th. century china. According to the inscription on its walls, it was restored after the 1665 fire by Sultan Mehmed IV. Ocaklı Sofa opens into the Head Haseki chamber. The Şehzadegan (The Princes' chamber) lies on top of the Head Haseki chamber. Through the Çeşmeli Sofa, we arrive at the Murad III's mansion.

The Mansion of Murad III:

One of the most adorable chambers of the Harem is the Murad III's mansion. It was built by Mimar Sinan in 1578 reflecting the splendour of the 16th. century. The whole chamber is covered with the coral red china scattered on the blue china ground. This splendid mansion is illuminated through the high windows. The chamber is covered by an impressive dome with classical ornaments on. The divans adorned with calligraphic art to the right are symmetrically placed.

The fireplace in the chamber reflects all the beauty of the era. Opposite the fireplace covered with copper, there lies an inset marble fountain which still runs. The reason why they used to leave the tap on most of the time was

to prevent others to overhear their conversation. Other significant works of art in that chamber are, the closets covered with mother-of-pearl, doors reflecting the splendour of the era, oriental sofas and the braziers. On the china, the walls have all around the hall is a verse from the Koran "Ayet-ül Kürsi". Beneath the mansion is a large pool. Let us move forward and reach Ahmed I's Library through the opposite door.

Ahmed I's Library:

This is a small chamber in a square shape adorned with the İznik China started to be produced after the china of Murad III's chamber. This place was built during the reign of Ahmed I by Sedefkar Mehmet Ağa. The library is adorable with its unique closets with a bull figure on covered with mother-of-pearl. To the left of the entrance, there lies a fountain in a niche dated 1608. The upper parts of the walls are covered with blue and white, green and white china going back to 17th. century. Yemiş odası, one of the smallest but the most remarkable rooms is located in this section.

Yemiş Odası(Fruit Room):

By the Ahmed I's chamber, Ahmed III's Has Oda was built in 1705. The room was adorned with calligraphic drawings of fruits in plates and flower bunches. In this square shaped room , the tourists are attracted by the mirror to the left, small niches, the fireplace covered with copper, small crystal candlesticks and the round copper tray on the ground. We can reach the Princes' chamber by the way we have taken to arrive here.

Twin Mansions-The Princes' Chamber:

After walking past the Murad III's mansion we can reach the Princes' chamber, so called the Twin Mansions. It consists of two rooms in one another accessible by a flight of steps. Those rooms were built by Murad IV and Mehmed IV. The first room belonged to Murad IV and is accessed by a narrow door. The room is almost in a square shape. Its dome is covered in golden gilded figures. That splendid dome had been hidden by a ceiling for long years. It suddenly appeared during a restoration work in the Harem. The side walls of the room are adorned with the impressive china of the 17th. century. The top of the fireplace to the left of the entrance was adorned with calligraphic art looking like china motives. There lies some inscriptions in between two windows as well as their interior parts. It has beautiful tiles all over and small taps in its windows. A tiny door leads you to the second room of the twin mansions.

That room is said to have been used by Mehmed IV. To the left of the room there lie a nice fireplace and a brazier to the right. This section has a ceiling with some geometric and plant motifs on and tiled windows. The closets covered with mother-of-pearl are on both sides of the fireplace. Its beauty is hard to narrate in black and white. Last restoration work caused an elevation difference on the ground floor. Those rooms both outside and inside which covered in china totally, were used by the crown Princes after the 18th. century.

The Favourites' Chamber:

After leaving the Princes' chamber where the Princes were either full of hopes or afraid of death once, you come across the Favourites' courtyard and the Favourites' pool. Down the way, is a place called Şimşirlik. The buildings seen behind the courtyard are the Favourites' chamber. The favourites' chamber has five separate rooms on the upper floors built by Abdülhamid I. The ground

The chamber of Princes built by two Sultans in the 17th. century, used by the crown princes of the Ottoman Dynasty.

Pictures from the first and the second rooms.

floor of that chamber belonged to the Sultan called the Sultan's yard with mirrors. From that room, the first room which is rather large is accessible by some hidden steps in a closet. The other rooms are smaller in comparison to that of the large one. You can reach there by stairs next to the golden path. And, finally we reach the corridor called the golden path.

The Golden Path:

46 meters in length, the golden path reminds you of a narrow street. Along that long road, the Concubines would satisfy their needs of going out.

The golden path witnessed some important incidents within the Ottoman history. As it is easily remembered, Cevri Kalfa stopped the traitors trying to kill Mahmud II by throwing ashes to their eyes from her brazier. It has no significant privileges apart from the Sultans' delivering golden coins at their Concubines on some special occasions.

The golden path is the last stop of the Harem which takes us to a charming world. We take the Kuşhane gate of the golden path to exit this mystic place.

In the second room of the princes chamber, cypress motif china panels and venetian blinds covered with mother-of-pearl.

The ornaments on the walls and ceilings of the princes chamber are eye-catching.

179

Select Bibliography

1. Çağatay Uluçay. Harem. T.T.K Basımevi Ankara 1971.

2. Çağatay Uluçay. Padişahların Kadınları ve Kızları, T.T.K Basımevi Ankara 1980.

3. Çağatay Uluçay. Osmanlı Saraylarında Harem Hayatının İç Yüzü, İnkilap Kitabevi İstanbul 1959

4. Çağatay Uluçay. Haremden Mektuplar, İstanbul Vakıf Matbaası,1956

5. Ord. Prof. İsmail Hakkı Uzunçarşılı. Osmanlı Devleti'nin Saray Teşkilatı. T.T.K. Basımevi, Ankara 1984

6. Prof. Dr. Ahmet Akgündüz. Osmanlı'da Harem. Osmanlı Araştırmaları Vakfı, İstanbul 1997

7. Prof. Dr. Yaşar Yücel-Prof. Dr. Ali Sevim. Türkiye Tarihi I.II.III. T.T.K. Basımevi, Ankara 1990

8. Enver Behnan Şapolyo. Osmanlı Sultanları Tarihi. Rıfat Zaimler. İst. 1961

9. Reşat Ekrem Koçu. Osmanlı Padişahları, Ana Yayınevi, İst. 1981

10. E.R. Toledano. Osmanlı Köle Ticareti., Tarih Vakfı, Yurt yayınları. İst. 1994

11. Ali Fuad Türkgeldi. Görüp İşittiklerim , T.T.K. Basımevi, Ankara 1984

12. Julia Pardoe.18. Yüzyılda İstanbul, İnkilap Kitabevi, İst. 1997

13. Sema Ok. Harem Ağaları, Kamer Yayınları, İst.1997

14. Burçak Evren-Dilek Girgin Can. Yabancı Gezginler ve Osmanlı Kadını. Milliyet Yay. İst. 1997

15. Godfrey Goodwin. Osmanlı Kadınının Özel Dünyası. Sabah Kitapları. İst. 1998

16. Antoine Galland. İstanbul'a Ait Günlük Anılar, T.T.K. Basımevi, Ankara 1973.

17. Yılmaz Öztuna. Büyük Türkiye Tarihi. Ötüken Yay. İst. 1978

18. Doç. Dr. Hasan Tahsin Fendoğlu. İslam ve Osmanlı Hukukunda Kölelik ve Cariyelik., Beyan Yay. İst. 1996

19. Mualla Anhegger-Eyüpoğlu. Topkapı Sarayı'nda Padişah Evi-Harem, Sandoz Yay. İst. 1987

20. Murat Bardakçı Şahbaba. Pan Yay. İst. 1998

21. Leslie P. Peirce. Harem-i Hümayun, Türk Vakfı Yurt Yayınları, İst. 1998

22. Alev Lytle Croutier. Harem, The World Behind The Veil, New York 1989

23. İlhan Akşit. The Topkapı Palace, Akşit Yay. 1994

24. Topkapı Sarayı. Akbank Yayınları, 2000

25. Carla Coco. Secrets of the Harem, Philip Wilson, London 1997